Play the Game

Badminton

Play the Game

Badminton

Pat Davis

WARD LOCK

Half title page: *Guo Xiong of China about to serve in the 1990 Asian Games*

Title page: *Celebration time! The winners of the mixed doubles at the 1994 All-England Championships at Birmingham, Jo Wright and Nick Ponting of England*

Above: *Ricky Subagdja and Rudy Gunawan of Indonesia during a rally in the World Badminton Championships at Birmingham in 1993*

Contents

Foreword

I am delighted to have been asked to prepare a foreword for this exciting new publication, and am pleased to give it my full support as President of the English Schools Badminton Association.

Badminton is smashing – those of us who have been around long enough need no convincing of that fact – and who are we to hog the finest of games? No, we like to share our enjoyment with *all* would-be wielders of a badminton racket.

In Ward Lock's new *Play the Game* series, badminton has been given an expert treatment by Pat Davis, the doyen of the badminton writing fraternity. A potted history of the game provides enough background to show that England was the motivator for this exciting and now worldwide game of badminton. (The Badminton Association of England celebrated its centenary in 1993.) This explanation of the origins of the game is followed by detailed information on all aspects of how to play the game. For the beginner, the descriptions are easy to understand, practical and not clouded with theory. The numerous illustrations are good and clear, and they reinforce all the descriptive points, from equipment to techniques. Once the beginner has had the appetite whetted in the opening sections of the book, and can appreciate the basics, then the finer techniques are presented to savour and ponder.

I wish all readers of this fine book success in developing skills which bring such personal enjoyment and satisfaction to all badminton players worldwide. They will need good speed and stamina in order to attain these, but this book explains how to get fit for badminton as well as how to play it. A final word: remember, as this book makes patently clear – for success, *keep it simple.*

Thomas A. Bowker
President of the English Schools Badminton Association
President of the Badminton Umpires Association of England
Honorary Vice-President of the Badminton
Association of England

History &
development of
badminton

Badminton is a fascinating game! One moment you are striking the shuttle with all your strength, the next you are stroking it delicately with millimetre accuracy.

At top level, badminton is the most demanding of racket games, calling for a fencer's speed of reflex and a gymnast's agility. And yet a beginner can have a fun game the first time he plays.

Its equipment of 100gm (3½ oz) racket and 5gm (⅙ oz) shuttle-cock (which for all its frailty can achieve 240km/h (150mph) off the racket) are marvels of modern precision engineering and aero-dynamics. And being so light they enable you to use very satisfying deception and to play the game to a ripe old age. I should know! After over fifty years' play, I still enjoy a game as much as ever.

Badminton's origins add a touch of glamour to the game. Its gentle forerunner, battledore and shuttlecock, in which the aim was

One of the English Schools Badminton Association logos

to keep a rally going, not to end it, was played in Ancient Greece and early Far Eastern civilizations (who sometimes used feet rather than rackets!). Medieval woodcuts show it being played with primitive, home-made rackets and shuttles. Nineteenth-century illustrations depict it as a languid game for the elegant and wealthy. And indeed it was played by the children of the Duke of Beaufort at his Gloucestershire mansion, Badminton House. If you visit it today you will be shown the crude battledore and big shuttles they used. On one of them is a remarkable inscription 'Kept up with Geraldine Somerset on Saturday 12th January to 2117. Henrietta Somerset'. Incredible concentration for a young girl. Try it yourself!

From those children's games it is thought that badminton was born. Army officers on leave from India with nothing better to do on a rainy day picked up the children's toys and played the first *competitive* game. A frequent visitor to Badminton House, John Lorraine Baldwin, may have devised the first crude laws as he had done for various card games. The first official rules were made in Poona, India, in 1877.

It was not until 1893 that the Badminton Association was formed with just fourteen clubs. They realized that the rules and court sizes varying in length from 13.4–18m (44–60ft) as well as shuttle speeds, ranging from cab-horse slow to rocket fast, must be standardized. By 1914 there were 467 clubs, in 1923, 550 clubs and by 1934 there were 1,000 clubs. Today there are some 5,000 affiliated clubs. And double that number of unaffiliated clubs who enjoy the benefits of a well-organized game but are loath to pay the small fees. Apart from these there are thousands of people playing individually at sports centres.

In 1934, the Badminton Association relinquished worldwide control of the fast growing game to the International Badminton Federation (IBF). It has continued, however, as the Badminton Association of England (BA of E), to do an excellent job in England of popularizing and improving the game at all levels from club to international. The All-England Championships, which have become badminton's Wimbledon and, unofficially, World Championships, started in 1899. After the IBF official World Championships, they are still the most prestigious and best organized championships in the world. Go to see them and watch the world's top players in thrilling action on Birmingham's National Exhibition Centre's seven fine courts. It's an unforgettable occasion!

On a lower level, in 1928/29, came the Inter-County Championships, the backbone of English badminton. Today, every county in England takes part; over a hundred I, II and III teams are put on court. In their own right, County Associations have done much to further the game in their own areas by forming leagues and running a wide range of tournaments which can be enjoyed by players of varied levels of skill. Don't miss out on these: they are great fun and a fine means of improving your play.

When life settled back to normal after World War II, the BA of E took another big step forward when they formed a Coaching Committee who organized courses for players, and for very necessary would-be coaches. Today, in addition to top flight coaches such as Steve Baddeley and Lee Joe Bok there are many hundreds of other trained coaches eager to help players at all levels in specially organized courses.

This coaching led to the emergence at an early age of such brilliant international players as Steve Baddeley himself and Darren Hall; Peter Knowles and Nick Ponting; Alison Humby and Joanne Wright. Although one of the strongest sides in Europe, England have not yet won major world individual or team championships. The meteoric rise first of Malaysia, then Indonesia, and now China has put paid to that.

The BA of E has done a tremendous job for English badminton. Similar excellent organizations are at work, largely voluntarily, in Wales, Ireland and Scotland.

The essential foundation of the game, the English Schools Badminton Association, must not be forgotten. This body, under the dedicated direction of Eric Brown and other volunteers, not only nurtures budding internationals but also teaches the game to tens of thousands of less brilliant youngsters to give them interest, exercise and fun for years to come.

Lastly, but not least, the International Badminton Federation. Today it controls the ever spreading game in currently over sixty countries from the Falklands to Kuwait, from Malaysia to America, from Malta to Mozambique. It organizes major events such as the individual World Championships as well as the two team Championships events, the Thomas Cup (men) and the Uber cup (Ladies), both named after famous English players. There is also a Grand Prix tournament which incorporates some fifteen other major tournaments played around the world. In this wide international scene names to remember are Morten Frost and Lene Köppen (Denmark); the Siddek brothers (Malaysia); Zhao Jianhua and Yang Yang (China); Rudy Hartono and Liem Swie King (Indonesia); Sumiko Kitada (Japan); Yun Ja Kim (South Korea). Names to conjure with today: Paul Hoyer-Larsen and T. Stuer Lauridsen (Denmark); Joki Suprianto and Susi Susanti (Indonesia); Ge Fei and Gu Jun (China); and many more world class players.

All of which goes to show that badminton has an exciting international flavour. However, for the moment all that concerns you is that almost immediately you will be able to play a simple game and let off steam, have fun and get plenty of exercise. In this country badminton is played indoors, but in some Asian countries where there are very still evenings, outdoors. (Don't try outdoors here unless you want the laugh of the century as you vainly try to hit a shuttle that veers disconcertingly away from your racket at the slightest breath of wind). It is therefore an ideal winter game that laughs at rain and fog, darkness and snow. But some enthusiasts do play through the summer as well. That's how badminton grabs you!

Have a good game, and keep on practising and learning. Above all *enjoy* it. Badminton is fun. I know!

Equipment & terminology

Before starting to learn how to play badminton, it is important to familiarize yourself with the equipment needed, and the terminology you will come across as you get to grips with the game.

EQUIPMENT

Avoid the twin evils of paying too little or too much for your equipment. But do buy the best you can afford. Good equipment does not necessarily make a good player but it certainly helps.

Rackets

Racket technology is changing all the time so get plenty of advice from the sales person helping you choose your racket before making your selection. You will not necessarily have to spend a lot of money, you can get a perfectly adequate racket to start with for a very affordable sum.

Handle Check that this is just the right and therefore comfortable size for you. The range of sizes from 8.6–9.2cm ($3\frac{3}{8}$–$3\frac{5}{8}$in) is seemingly small but choose one that feels neither too small so that you cannot hold it effectively, or too big so that you hold it too tightly. Make sure it has a grip on it that lives up to its name even when your hands are damp. Leather is best; towelling tends to become matted.

Shaft The material varies with price, ranging from tempered steel to graphite, graphite and fibreglass, graphite and boron, and recently graphite and ceramic fibre. Do not be bewildered by this list – steel will do, graphite, with additives, gives ever greater durability and lightness. 100gm (3½ oz) is the right weight.

Whichever you choose it should have whip, i.e. bend slightly. To test this, hold the racket horizontally by the top of the head with one hand and at the end of the handle with the other. Press upwards *gently* (no snapped shafts in the shop, please!) and the shaft should flex slightly.

The racket

Head This again may be graphite and its additives, or aluminium. Avoid an all-steel head, which tends to be cumbersome and ill-balanced. It should be 'channelled' so that the strings are not scraped if you scoop up a shuttle from the floor. To prevent the strings rubbing against the metal frame and fraying, see that the holes are lined with soft plastic protectors, i.e. grommets.

T-piece The head and shaft, if of graphite, etc. are moulded in one piece. If metal, they are joined by a T-piece. This join is known as the throat. In a very few models it may be 'open', to save weight.

Strings Most important of all, since they provide the impetus to enable you to hit a shuttle hard and fast, are the strings. Natural gut is the best. It has more resilience than synthetic gut – and is correspondingly more expensive. The best such gut is clear and thin. The best synthetic guts are either oil-filled or multi-minuscule (filled with microscopic fibres).

Whichever you choose its tensioning is vitally important. If it is too tight, especially with synthetic guts, it is difficult to control or 'feel' the shuttle in delicate strokes; if too slack, it is difficult to hit hard. Normally strings should be tensioned at about 5.9kg (13lb).

Two basic tension tests are these. Flick your fingernail lightly across the strings – they should gave a crisp 'ping'. And if you hold your racket head with the thumbs on either side of the frame and press the stringing with them it should give – *very* slightly.

Care To get the best out of your carefully chosen racket, take care of it. Never throw or bounce it on the floor in bad temper. Use a head-cover to ensure the strings do not get wet. Expose the racket neither to heat nor damp. Treated carefully it should give you good service for two or three years before needing a restring. If a string snaps do not continue to use it or further damage will result. Have it repaired immediately to maintain tension.

Shuttles

Badminton's 'ball' is the fragile and aerodynamically efficient shuttle-cock. It weighs an average of 4.8g i.e. roughly 6 to an ounce!

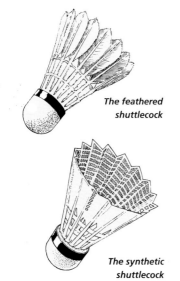

The feathered shuttlecock

The synthetic shuttlecock

Feathered and synthetic There are two types: the original feathers, and the comparatively recently-invented substitute, the synthetic. Both have a domed base of cork or polyurethane containing the tiny lead weight without which the shuttle would be too light to fly the necessary distances. To this is attached the 'skirt', in one case of sixteen feathers, in the other, a synthetic material.

Top players play only with feathered shuttles. Synthetic shuttles are perfectly acceptable for beginners and most club players. 'Gold' coloured synthetics are a good choice in halls with light backgrounds. And 'cold' synthetics last longer in cold weather. Prices (Synthetic £7 to £10 per dozen; feathered £7 to £12 per dozen) and durability vary widely. Considerable savings can be made by dealing with the numerous mail order firms who advertise regularly in the BA of E official magazine, *Badminton*.

Feathered shuttles were once far more expensive than synthetic; today, some brands are no more or even less expensive than synthetic ones. Make sure, however, if you opt for them, that the feathers are strong goose feathers. Base your choice on price, tested durability, and the type used by your friends or club. It is not advisable to switch from one type to the other. Here again, great names count: RSL, DSS, Carlton, Yonex.

Correct speed Whichever shuttles you choose make sure they are tested for the correct speed needed in your hall. Some shuttles, generally synthetic, are colour-graded 'slow', 'medium' and 'fast'. Virtually all feathered shuttles are numerically graded from 73 to 85. These figures indicate the weight – in grains (a grain = 0.065g) – and therefore the speed. A 73 will travel some 10–15cm (4–6in) less distance than a 74, and so on, with 85s being the fastest.

The speed you should use depends on the size and temperature of the hall you play in – in other words, on the air-resistance. In a small, heated, one-court hall you might use a 75, while if it was unheated, a 78; in cavernous, modern sports centres you might need an 82.

Once you can hit effectively, find out for yourself the correct speed by the following test. Holding the shuttle *directly over the base-line* hit it hard, underhand, straight, at an upward angle of 45°. If it is the correct speed, it will drop not less than 0.53m (1ft 9in) (too fast) and not more than 1.0m (3ft 3in) (too slow) short of the other back boundary line.

Care A shuttle's life, especially when mis-hit, is all too short – and expensive. So treat them with loving care!
1 Never hit them on the half-volley.
2 Don't crush or bang their container.
3 Never store feathered shuttles in heat.
4 Always smooth ruffled plumes between thumb and forefinger.
5 Play with the correct speed.

Shoes

What you wear on your feet is far more important than what you wear on your body. Shoes are the foundation of all-important speed. They should be as light and *flexible* as is possible commensurate with having some interior cushioning. A soft but rough or ridged sole (not black) is essential for the grip needed for stopping, starting and turning. Nylon and suede are often used in the uppers. The lacing should be grommeted and from toe to instep, and the tongue lightly padded. A padded, heel tab support may mitigate against Achilles tendon trouble. Strong toe-guard and toe-cap are essential to prevent wear by dragging the foot.

Heavy, hard soled trainers are the last thing you should wear if speed and balance are your aim. Dirty shoes betoken a sloppy player. So keep them clean – and fresh!

Clothing

This is largely a matter of personal preference. Many very attractive outfits are available. Men wear shorts, shirt and sweater; ladies, the same, but with the alternatives of skirt, dress or cardigan. The colour should be predominantly white and of modern fashion; using colour sparingly but effectively is permissible. White socks too of course.

Garments should be short, of absorbent and easily washed material, and never so tight or long as to restrict movement. Off-court a track-suit is a useful adjunct that will keep you warm after a hard game and so help prevent pulled muscles. Never play in one except perhaps in the knock-up; it looks sloppy and hampers easy action. Give thought to your clothes. 'Whites' are not essential for informal school or sports centre knockabouts. But whatever you wear, if you look smart and attractive you will look and *feel* like a player.

Badminton clothing

Off-court bag

Once you play in matches or tournaments, an off-court bag can be a wise provision. As play must be continuous, it should cater for all emergencies: an extra racket of the same weight and tension as that generally used, safety pins, sweat-bands, towel, a salted glucose drink, talc for sweaty hands, spectacles demisting agent (assuming you wear them, that is!), elastoplasts, hair bandeau – and a copy of the Laws for a friendly settlement of any disputes.

The court

The accompanying diagrams speak louder than words in regards to names and distances. Obviously, to be able to communicate, you must know the former and it is helpful and advisable to know the latter.

An ideal court will have a clear height of 9.1m (30ft), be marked out with lines 3.8cm (1½in) wide and be 1.52m (5ft) at least from a back wall and 0.9m (3ft) from a neighbouring court. For good sighting of the shuttles, daylight should be without glare; artificial light, above the posts, without dazzle. Background walls should be a matt dull green. The floor should be smooth but not slippery. Posts are set *on* the outside lines so as to keep the net taut: 1.54m (5ft 1in) near the post and 1.52m (5ft) in the centre. These measurements are taken from the floor to the top of the net.

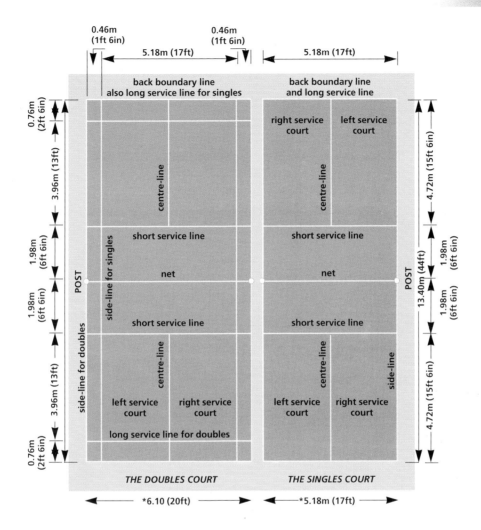

0.46m (1ft 6in) 0.46m (1ft 6in)

5.18m (17ft)   5.18m (17ft)

0.76m (2ft 6in)

3.96m (13ft)

1.98m (6ft 6in)

1.98m (6ft 6in)

3.96m (13ft)

0.76m (2ft 6in)

4.72m (15ft 6in)

1.98m (6ft 6in)

1.98m (6ft 6in)

4.72m (15ft 6in)

13.40m (44ft)

POST

POST

back boundary line
also long service line for singles

back boundary line
and long service line

right service court   left service court

centre-line   centre-line

short service line   short service line

net   net

short service line   short service line

centre-line   centre-line

left service court   right service court

left service court   right service court

long service line for doubles

side-line for singles

side-line for doubles

side-line

THE DOUBLES COURT   THE SINGLES COURT

*6.10 (20ft)   *5.18m (17ft)

Sadly very few courts live up to these ideals. But badminton is still played – and enjoyed – in much more difficult 'rabbit-hutch' conditions where a strong backswing results in a snapped racket, and the luckless shuttle has to traverse a maze of low beams, lights and heaters in glare or gloom!

* Measurements include line widths

Where to play

Schools and clubs obviously have their own courts. As the latter are chary of accepting complete beginners, there are two options:

1 Book a court, with a friend, at your local sports centre.

2 Join an Adult Study Centre evening class where you will also get tuition. If still in doubt ask at your local newspaper office or local sports outfitters shop.

TERMINOLOGY

Angled drive serve The idea of all serves is to try and 'con' your opponent. The angled drive is a 'con' of a 'con' – the drive. For the angled drive serve you stand as far to the right of the service court as you can within the laws, and then kid your opponent into thinking you are going to serve a low serve but then make it a drive. Standing to the right of the service court will give you that extra width to play across court.

Attacking clear An advanced overhead attacking stroke, hit low and fast to the back line of your opponent's court.

Backhand low serve The same as the low serve, but played on the backhand. The high or very high serve are never played on the backhand, and the drive serve only infrequently.

Bird Another name for the shuttlecock.

Danish wipe (or Swedish swish). A cross between a drive and a lob.

Defensive clear The more commonly-used defensive version of the attacking clear. It is an overhead stroke hitting the shuttle high from one base-line to the other.

Drive serve This is another 'disguised serve'. It appears to be a standard low serve but at the last moment the racket-head is speeded up and the serve driven to a part of the opposing court where you know your opponent is at his weakest.

Flick serve To all intents and purposes this serve looks like a low serve to your opponent, but at the very last minute you uncock your wrist and slightly loft the shuttle, which will go towards the back of the court and, hopefully, catch your opponent unawares.

Forehand smash An attacking stroke. The object is to hit the shuttle down as fast and as steeply over the net as possible. There is also a backhand version.

High serve A serve played with such loft that it forces your opponent to the back of the court. It blunts his smash, and opens up the front of the court.

Let When a point has to be replayed a 'let' is called.

Lob A defensive forehand or backhand stroke, played underhand and used to return a shuttle which is well below tape-level, in the forecourt, high to the base-line.

Low serve A delicate serve that starts to dip before crossing the tape. It is the 'bread and butter' serve and if played accurately forces a 'lift' because the receiver cannot play down on to the shuttle.

Net-shots A variety of shots played *from* near the net and often very near *to* the net.

Overhead drop-shot A deceptive shot, disguised as a smash, but just gently dropped over the net. If it is not a winning shot it will have drawn your opponent near to the net. Used more in singles than doubles.

Rush A fast movement forward by the receiver to dab the shuttle aggressively down for a winner.

Swedish swish See *Danish wipe*.

Tape The white tape at the top of the net.

Very high serve Similar to a high serve, but hit as high as your strength, and the roof, allow, to make timing difficult for your opponent.

The game –
a guide

Badminton can be played as singles or doubles, either men's, women's or mixed. The shuttlecock must not hit the ground during a rally or the rally is lost.

The Rules of Badminton

Most matches consist of the best-of-three games. A game is won by the first player or pair to reach 15 points (11 in ladies singles).

Like squash, in badminton it is only the server who can win points. In singles, if the non-server wins the rally then he becomes the server and has the chance to score points thereafter. In doubles, both players of a side serve before the service changes sides.

Commencing a game and serving

The players toss a coin or spin a racket to decide who shall serve first. Serving is done diagonally and the first serve is from the right-hand service court. The server alternates between the right and left service courts until the serve is lost. When the new server takes his first serve, it is always from the service court that he is then in.

When a pair regains the serve from its opponents, the first serve is always from the right-hand service court.

In doubles play, each side has two 'chances' with the serve. If they lose the rally on the first serve they do not pass the service to the opposing side, but instead the second member of the team serves. If they lose the rally on **his** serve though, they **do** lose the serve. At the start of a doubles game however, the initial pairing is allowed **only** one service chance.

In doubles, it is the serving pair who alternate between service courts, not the receiving pair. They stay put. In singles play, both players change sides for every new service. If the server's score is an odd number, 1, 3, 5, etc., then service commences in, and to, the left service court; if it is even, 2, 4, 6, etc., the right.

The server must stand entirely within the service court and with part of **both** feet on the ground. The shuttle must be hit underarm and the racket must make contact with it below the server's waist. The receiving player must be in the court diagonally opposite and must also have part of both feet on the ground. Once the serve has been returned, players may move around at random. In doubles play, the players do not have to play the shuttle in sequence, as in table tennis. Badminton is a very much more flexible game in this respect.

Setting

Once the scores reach 13-all in all disciplines (except ladies singles), the match can be set to 5. This means the first player (or team) who reached 13, after it became 13-all, can either carry on to 15 as if nothing had happened or opt to play a further 5 points, i.e. until one side scores 5 points. If one side wins, say, 5-3, a score of 18-16 is registered, not 5-3.

The same setting option is open once the scores reach 14-all, but this time the game can be only set to 3.

In ladies singles setting is to 3 at 9-all or to 2 at 10-all.

Setting is not allowed in handicap games.

Changing ends

Ends are changed at the completion of each game, and if the match goes to a deciding game ends are changed when one player or pair reaches 8. In ladies' singles the change is made at 6.

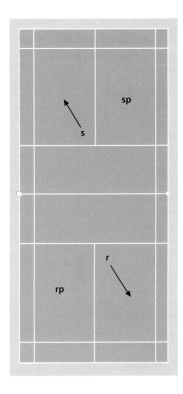

OPENING POSITIONS: BEGINNING A GAME OF DOUBLES

s = server
sp = server's partner
r = receiver
rp = receiver's partner
———▶ *= movement*

The rally

The rally continues until one player makes a fault. There are a number of ways he can do this. The most common by far are:

(a) Missing the shuttle completely

(b) Failing to hit it over the net

(c) Hitting it into the net

(d) Hitting it outside the court boundary lines, either in service or in play

(e) Touching the net either with his body or racket while the shuttle is in play

(f) Hitting the shuttle twice in succession with two strokes.

Other much less common faults are dealt with in the **Rules Clinic**.

Scoring

Some people believe scoring in badminton to be difficult; well, it isn't! If you remember the following, scoring is easy:

(a) When the serving side win a rally, they add a point to their score; when they lose a rally, they lose one player's serve

(b) When the receiving side win a rally, they do not get a point but they have taken one of their opponents' serves away; when they lose a rally their opponents gain a point.

One player should be elected to call the score aloud at the end of each rally. The score starts at 0-0, called 'love-all'. The serving side's score is called first. If they win the rally and lead 1-0, that is the score called. If they lose the next rally it is then the turn of the second player to serve. The score is called '1-0 second server', '2-0 second server', and so on.

When a rally is lost and service passes to the other side, the score is called as, say, 0-2. When it passes to the second server it is '0-2 second server'. Always put the serving side's score first.

Right – you've learnt the rules, and hopefully you now under-stand scoring and setting. If you don't, then read them again. When you get on court, you should, at the earliest opportunity, take upon yourself the task of scoring. That is the best way to learn. You will make mistakes, but, let's face it, it is really the only way to learn properly.

Stretching for a shot at the 1996 Yonex All-England Championships

Rules
clinic

Answering your questions on
points of the rules.

Can I do an overhead Boris Becker serve at badminton?
No. This would be a fault for two reasons: (a) at impact all, not
merely part of the shuttle would be well above the top of the hip-
bone and (b) the racket-head would also be clearly above the hand
holding it. Both heinous badminton crimes.

**When serving, can I pretend to hit the shuttle one way – then hit it
the other?**
Yes, provided that the racket is in *continuous* motion throughout.
With the same proviso, you can deceptively speed up or slow down
the movement of the racket.

**If the shuttle when served strikes the net-cord, can I claim a 'let' or
replay as in tennis?**
No, there are no 'lets' for this in badminton, so the shuttle should
be played. It is, however, a fault if the shuttle actually stays on the
tape, or is caught in the net on the receiver's side – but it's a million-
to-one chance! During a rally, such an occurrence would be a 'let'.

You say 'Don't hurry when serving or taking up a receiving stance'.

How long am I allowed?
There must be no *undue* delay. Say seven seconds?

If I anticipate my opponent's serve may I move to intercept it before he actually hits the shuttle?
No, it is a fault to move before his shuttle is struck.

What happens if a server serves before I'm ready?
Provided you make no attempt to play it you can claim a let.

What happens if I hit the shuttle over the net on the head or shaft?
Provided it is one clean hit, it is quite legal. It is, however, a fault if you 'sling' the shuttle, i.e. hit the shuttle in a curving trajectory after 'holding' it momentarily on your racket (probably between frame and strings). You must declare such a fault yourself.

If I see an opponent is going to kill a shot at the net may I protect my face with my racket?
Yes, provided you do not baulk or distract him by waving the racket about.

What happens if I miss the shuttle altogether or just touch it when serving?
The shuttle has not crossed the net so it is a fault.

Does it matter if I hit the net in my follow through?
It is a fault. So too, if during play, you touch the net in any way, put a foot under it, slide bodily under it, or let your racket fly over it. You have invaded your opponent's court.

If a shuttle hits only the outside edge of a line is it 'in' or 'out'?
The lines bounding a court are 'in', no matter how little of them is touched. Though conversely, if, when serving or receiving, you stand, even fractionally, on a line, your foot is *outside* the court: a fault.

SERVICE FAULTS
What an horrific picture! Four foul serves in one! Can you spot them?

Can I jump to play a shot?
By all means, except when you are serving or waiting to receive. Then you must have part of each foot in contact with the floor in the service court opposite your opponent. Conversely you may play a shot when lying on the floor; some players can do it.

Can I hit the shuttle before it is on my side of the net?
No. To do so is a fault because, if left, your opponent's shot might have been too tight to the net for you to return. You may however follow through over the net provided you have first struck the shuttle on your side.

If I hit the shuttle or am hit by it when I'm standing outside the line, may I still claim the shuttle is 'out'?
No. whether you are 'in' or 'out' of the court and are hit by the shuttle, it is a fault.

Do we play on if the shuttle just grazes my hair, my racket or my clothing before my partner hits the shuttle?
You must declare a 'touch' even though, as a fault, it loses you the rally.

What do we do if a shuttle touches a roof beam or girder?
Clubs have their own rules on this. Generally, hitting a girder results in a 'let'. Hitting the roof itself is a fault as this could be done deliberately when in difficulties.

May I stop in a game or between games to get my wind back or to get advice from my coach?
No. Play must be continuous.

What is the position if the shuttle is badly damaged in mid-rally?
Play continues unless 'skirt' and base part company completely, when a 'let' would be played.

Are these all the Laws?
All you need to start with. The full Laws can be bought very cheaply at sports outfitters or obtained from the Badminton Association of England, whose address appears on page 78.

Taking the shuttle too early

Joanne Muggeridge of England reaches high to return during the Commonwealth Games team event in 1994

Technique

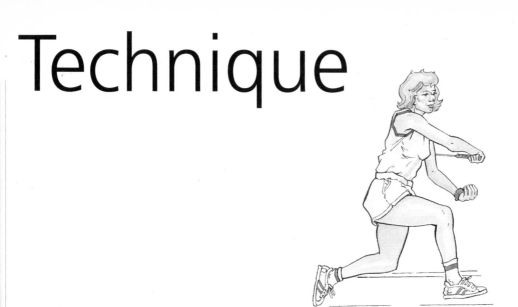

Badminton is a very physical game demanding quick movement and hard hitting with only a matter of seconds between long rallies.

It is therefore important to realize that in every stroke several parts of the body must synchronize to produce an effective shot.

All power strokes are a form of throwing. By uncocking your wrist just before impact (usually just in front of the body) the racket-head is moving at its fastest in the 'zip' or 'zing' area (46cm (18in) either side of impact). Perfect timing results.

Eye

The old maxim 'keep your eye on the shuttle' is still a valid one. Pick up its line of flight immediately it leaves your opponent's racket and watch the shuttle on to the very strings of your own racket.

When hitting upwards, keep you head down for a fraction *after* impact. If you look up just before impact, thinking you can't miss it – you may well do so.

Fast feet

In a game played over a 1.52m (5ft) net and with a 'ball' that is not allowed to bounce (even if it could!), it is impossible to overstate the need for speed of movement and good balance. And on a small half-court, only 6.1 x 6.7m (20 x 22ft), badminton movement is a series of short, sharp movements of no more than four of five paces. These involve good braking, quick starting, bending, stretching, turning, jumping and last second changes of direction – almost an acrobat's routine. Even if you are only a split second slow in meeting the shuttle, you may have lost the chance to attack!

Exercises for speed Strong legs and ankles help to give initial and essential acceleration. Exercises, such as step-ups, squat-jumps, bunny hops, star-jumps and skipping, both for lightness and power, will help.

Observation plays its part Equally important as a fast start is an early start. You will get to the shuttle earlier than a faster runner who doesn't move until it is practically crossing the net. To this end you must train yourself to 'read' what kind of stroke your opponent is playing almost as the shuttle leaves his racket.

Anticipation Try to decide, even before the shuttle is hit, what will be your opponent's *likely* shot. After an angled drive serve to your opponent's backhand, anticipate a weak return to the net. With the shuttle behind your slow-moving opponent in rear court expect a short clear. After a smash into the body expect a cramped return lacking power. You will see these results more often than not. Also remember that most players are creatures of habit.

Position of readiness Even for the split-second between strokes, quickly position yourself roughly centrally to avoid leaving gaps. From such a base you want a good springboard for movement. This is your 'position of readiness', the stance you immediately take up after each stroke as you regain base.

When you are attacking, you should be upright, knees slightly bent, turned slightly sideways to the net with your left foot in advance, and *on the balls of your feet*. The latter point is of prime importance.

Your feet should never be still or your body weight inertia tends to become greater, and it is therefore harder to drive into swift action. Either do a little shuffle or bounce to reduce it.

Perfect body control – everything synchronized for an ideal stroke: good balance; knees bent; body leaning into stroke; elbow bent; correct grip; early and full backswing; eyes on the shuttle

The perfect position for readiness

Your racket too must be equally ready. Since you are hoping to attack, hold it at *head height* slightly forward of the body. When you are defending – that is, when you have hit the shuttle upwards – expect a hit down. So lower the racket so that it is across a likely target, your stomach. Feet are still on the move but you may prefer a rather squarer stance with the right foot slightly forward.

Actual movement This should be light and well-balanced. Moving forward from a base-line to net you will run; moving backwards you can either run or chassé (skipping sideways, bringing one foot up to the other); the former is preferable as it is slightly faster.

Braking, acceleration and balance Good 'braking' and recovery are equally essential. Running forward to the net generally ends in a long lunge, an action with three advantages. It reaches forward, so saving another short step, it is an excellent means of braking, and the outstretched right foot provides an effective push-off in recovery. This also applies to sideways movement. In running backwards, a final longer backward step has the advantages of the lunge. Short steps are best for initial acceleration and for instant, driving recovery.

Balance, so easily lost by a late start and stumbling move-ment, is also very important; good balance saves steps!

THE LUNGE

Killer instinct Finally, yet another facet of speed. You must have in you the 'killer' instinct that sends you leaping to the shuttle at the slightest possibility of a winner. And, equally, the 'never-say-die' instinct that sends you stretching, even diving to the floor, if that is going to prevent the shuttle hitting it, and the point being lost.

So use head, heart and eye as well as feet and legs to move fast. Never be slack and sluggish, unaware and unalert. Never, never just stand back and let a shuttle come to you. Always go fast to meet the shuttle early, above the tape. Then, the points will come.

Killer instinct!

Arm

This is the obvious generator of racket-head speed. In all power shots it must be fully bent and strongly *snapped straight* with a vigorous throwing action; never, never just pushed forward. To its speed are added those of wrist and forearm.

Forearm

Modern thinking is that the turn of the forearm is responsible for much power. When a right-hander raises his racket-head and then drops it over his shoulder into the small of his back, the forearm turns from left to right. In the actual hitting it should *pronate* strongly, i.e. turn back from right to left.

In backhand shots the opposite takes place. In the actual hitting action when the forearm turns from left to right, it *supinates*. Try it for extra power!

Wrist

This is the vital partner of the arm. Notice, with racket in hand, how it can be bent backwards ('cocked'), or forwards ('uncocked') explosively, it can also be turned to the right and to the left.

The wrist is used in every power stroke. Thereby it holds the threat of explosive power, for when it is uncocked, wrist speed is added to arm speed.

A last-second turn of the wrist is equally effective. This time it provides deception, for the shuttle which was apparently going to be played to the forehand is now turned to the backhand or vice versa. And, by keeping the uncocking of the wrist back to the last split second, 'holding', and then suddenly employing it with a slow arm action the speed *and* trajectory of the shuttle can be altered bewilderingly at the last moment.

Body

In all power strokes, body weight is on the back foot at the end of the preparation. It must, in the course of the stroke, be swung forwards, by turning hips and shoulders, into the line of flight of the shuttle, with the body square to the net at impact.

This thrusting of almost total bodyweight into the stroke can add considerable power. So never be afraid to bend the body backwards and turn the shoulders into a side-on position. From that position, the body weight should be spiralled upwards into overhead strokes.

For control and balance, rather than power, the same is done, much more gently, even in low serve and net-shot. In the former, the body-turn on its own is nearly enough to hit the shuttle the short distance needed. In the lob, a little more body swing is needed. In backhand drives and Danish wipes the body turn should be strongly added to the flinging of the racket.

STROKE TECHNIQUES

The grip

Get the grip right and you're likely to get most of your strokes right. There are two simple ways of obtaining the correct grip. In the first get someone to hold your racket by the head and extend the handle towards you sideways on and horizontally. Then, simply shake hands with it … after all it's going to be your best friend, isn't it? In the second way, simply place your racket flat on the ground, then pick it up, sideways on, as if it were an axe.

In each case you should notice the four following points:

1 The V between thumb and forefinger is in line with the shaft.
2 Your fingers are slightly spaced apart, especially the forefinger from the second finger.
3 The butt end of the racket nestles just within the palm of your hand to give you maximum reach and leverage.

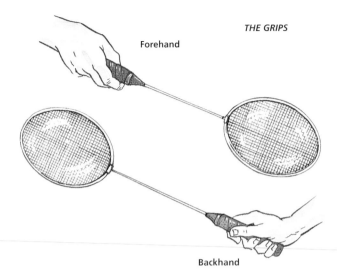

THE GRIPS

Forehand

Backhand

Frying-pan

4 If you turn your hand to the right, palm upwards, and open it, you will see that the racket lies across the base of your *fingers,* rather than your palm. This will give you control, feel and touch. A racket as light as this should be held like a surgical scalpel.

This is your basic grip with which all strokes can be played. The special grips for backhand strokes and net-shots will be explained when those strokes are described.

In the basic grip your racket-head is sideways on to the shuttle. Don't worry! Your wrist will naturally turn the racket face square to the shuttle at impact. But do make sure you do this by turning your wrist – not by turning the racket handle in your hand. This will give you what for obvious reasons is called a 'frying-pan grip'. In its wake it generally brings a square stance and a weak dabbing action. That's a badminton crime! You have been warned!

Do keep checking your grip to ensure you avoid this pitfall. Remember also not to hold the racket too loosely or too tightly. In the former case you will lack power, touch and control. In the latter, zip and a flexible and deceptive wrist.

The serves

Badminton, like tennis, can boast a wide and exciting variety of serves. The Laws of Badminton are particularly restrictive where the serve is concerned. They effectively outlaw brute strength and force

SERVE TRAJECTORIES
1 low serve
2 drive serve
3 flick serve
4 high serve
5 very high serve

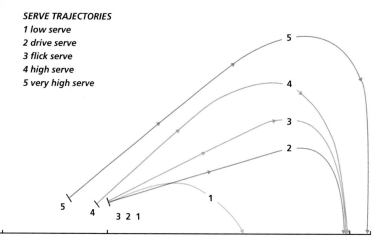

THE ACTION FOR THE HIGH SERVE

the server to rely on millimetre accuracy – and trickery.

They are too, unfortunately, one of the game's few bones of contention, because the difference between 'fair' and 'foul' is minimal and extremely difficult to discern. At club level the Laws are often flouted – out of ignorance rather than intent. So restrain your natural impatience and first re-read the rules. (See page 20).

High serve The aim of the high serve is to force your opponent back in court and to blunt his attack. However, be wary of using this serve against experienced players with strong smashes.

To play the stroke, stand sideways on with your left shoulder and foot pointing into the diagonally opposite court. For doubles, you base is near the centre-line and up to a couple of feet behind the front service line. By way of preparation, hold the shuttle, between thumb and forefinger, with outstretched arm at shoulder height, so that if dropped it would fall a foot outside your leading foot, the left one. Sway backwards so that your weight is on the back foot. With arm bent and wrist cocked, the racket is held up almost vertically behind and to the right of your thigh. Choose your target area, then simply open thumb and forefinger to allow the shuttle to drop straight, sweeping the racket down to meet it, with the heel of the hand leading, the arm straightening, the body turning square to the net, and the knees bending slightly.

Some 0.5cm (18in) before impact give the arm a final accelera-tion and uncock your wrist so that at impact you are hitting hard,

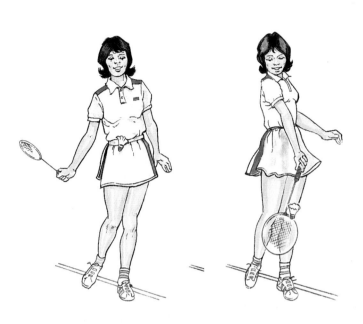

upwards, on a line with that in-the-mind's eye target area. Keeping on that line, make a long sweep of the racket forward, up and above the left shoulder. Recover to an alert position of defensive readiness.

Do be relaxed and confident, not rigid and desperate. You're hitting the shuttle only some 9m (30ft) so there's no need to 'belt' it – just swing easily. Above all do make sure that your racket-head is under firm control at impact.

The low serve Against experienced players with hard smashes an alternative to the high serve must be found. This is the low serve, the bread and butter serve of the game.

The aim of the low serve is to strike the shuttle with the flattest possible trajectory, so that it starts to drop just before crossing and literally skimming the tape and therefore cannot be hit down. The need for such millimetre accuracy? Not yet, but in years to come, your receiver will be standing toe to service line with racket held high menacingly within 1.5m (5ft) of the tape. With a single lunge he can demolish a still rising shuttle. So learn how to keep it low!

As with the high serve, stand sideways on, facing the receiver

THE LOW SERVE

diagonally. So, with left foot and shoulder forward, stand tall, weight slightly on the back foot. Hold the shuttle's skirt at the top between the forefinger and thumb with arm bent so that when released the shuttle will drop just to the right of your leading foot.

With the right hand, hold the racket in the conventional grip. Ensure that your grip is relaxed – not too tight and not too loose. Place your racket, pointing downwards, just to the right of and slightly behind the right thigh. No power is needed so a longer backswing is not required. Bend the arm as far as you comfortably can to bring the racket-head up vertically as high as possible. This will give you a flatter trajectory. And the wrist is firmly cocked back – *and kept cocked back throughout the stroke.* Now, choose your target area, relax and take your time.

Looking only at the shuttle, sway forward and gently but firmly, arm bent, wrist still cocked, *push* the shuttle forward. Don't *hit* it – stroke it, coax it. Impact is made just below hip height. With the shuttle now irretrievably on its way, step forward, and raise your racket intimidatingly tape-high. You are ready to deal with any quick return to the net. Don't forget to practise this as it is, after all, the foundation of your game.

The flick serve 'But if I always serve low, won't my opponent anticipate it?' I hear you say. Dead right! He will. So you must have a
surprise up your sleeve so that he is never quite certain. That
surprise is the 'flick' – a last fraction-of-a-second, crisp lofting of the
shuttle instead of yet another low serve. Hopefully it will wrong-
foot your opponent, forcing a weak, smashable return or even
score an outright glorious winner.

   The action? It must be a surprise, a look-alike, if it is to
survive. So it is played in every way *exactly* like the low service. But,
a foot – no more – before impact, the wrist you kept so unfalter-
ingly locked back to secure a flat trajectory in the low serve, is
crisply uncocked. The shuttle rises – but only just high enough to
escape the unraised racket – and drops near the back doubles
service line. The low service is played with the wrist cocked back
throughout; the 'flick' *with* a flick of the wrist.

The drive serve This is another variant of the low serve for sparing
and surprise use. Its aim is to hit the shuttle fast, and as flat as the
Laws permit, into a gap or at a vulnerable target such as the face or
a weak backhand in the right court. So once again it is played
exactly like the low serve until just a foot before impact when the
slow moving right hand is suddenly speeded up. But to keep the
trajectory flattish, and so less vulnerable, the wrist must be kept
cocked back as in the low serve.

The angled drive serve This is a variant of a variant . . . of the drive
serve. To gain a still wider angle, move your serving base from near
the centre-line to the doubles side-line. Place your feet carefully, so
that you are not infringing the rules by standing on a line. The right
foot is placed right up to it, the left, a little further forward and
away from it. Again, your left shoulder points to the diagonally
opposite corner. The shuttle is, however, held as far out over the
side-line as is consistent with remaining on balance. This gives you a
still wider angle of attack. Once again, simply jab towards the
backhand target areas – powerfully.

The very high serve Your aim with this serve is to hit the shuttle as
high as strength and roof allow. To do this simply employ the
technique already outlined for the high serve but use your wrist

THE BACKHAND SERVE

rather more fiercely and sweep rather more strongly upwards, using body-turn to the full. Falling vertically, the shuttle will be more difficult to time and hit cleanly.

Backhand low serve Neither the high nor the very high serve are often played backhanded, the drive serve only infrequently. So forget them. Do, however, remember and practise the backhand low serve – and flick too, of course. They must always be considered together, for one without the other is of little use.

As with all backhand strokes, use the backhand grip, thumb *behind* the handle, and point the right foot forward – right up to the front service line. The left is a little behind and to one side. Hold the shuttle, arm straight, at about 45° just below the top of your hip, well in front of your stomach. With right arm well bent and wrist cocked, place the racket-head vertically, immediately behind the shuttle. Your elbow is high. It may seem a little awkward but you'll soon get used to it. Backswing completed.

Now, relax and select your target area, as usual. Then draw the racket back as long or as short a distance as you like – right back to your body or a matter of mere inches. Without pause, your backswing becomes your forward swing, though 'push' is again a more accurate description. Simply extend the bent forearm, *keeping the wrist cocked*, to make contact with the shuttle 0.5m (18in) in front of the body, just below hip height. Follow through quite gently for just a foot or so to dispatch the shuttle on its net-skimming way. Then, smartly, bend the arm upwards to bring the racket-head to tape level and move in to the net. There are four distinct advantages to this serve:

1 The shuttle is struck 0.5m (18in) in front of the front service line not 0.6m (2ft) behind it: a saving of nearly 1.2 in valuable metres (4ft). This gives your opponent some 20 per cent less time to move in to attack.
2 White shuttle held directly in front of white sweater is more difficult to spot quickly than white shuttle held slightly to one side.
3 The forward swing is very short and the margin of error reduced.
4 Even today, quite a number of players have not seen it. Consequently, it holds a certain daunting threat.

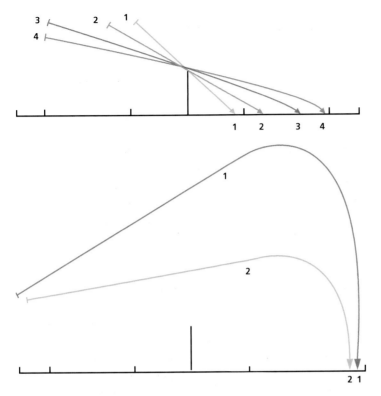

TRAJECTORIES OF SMASHES
1 from net
2 from mid-court
3 from doubles back service line,
   steeply angled
4 too flat and deep

TRAJECTORIES OF CLEARS
1 defensive
2 attacking

Backhand flick serve Strangely, this, unless you have a strong wrist, is the one snag with the backhand serve if played with a short backswing! A weak wrist will make it impossible to achieve suffi-cient height to escape early interception. A longer backswing and an average wrist should just do the trick.

Once again, for deception, the flick must be played exactly like the low serve. Remember, whatever backswing you have for one you must have for the other. Remember too, the added power needed, as with the forehand version, must stem solely from late wrist action not early, and not from easily detectable, faster or longer arm action. Follow through is minimal and recovery quick.

Forehand overhead strokes

Since points are rarely won by just hitting the shuttle upwards, and since badminton sports a 1.5m (5ft) high net compared with the 0.9m (3ft) one of tennis and the 48cm (19in) high 'tin' of squash, the majority of shots are played overhead. It is therefore essential that you are strong in this branch of the game. And the good news is that if you can *throw* as opposed to *push* you are off to a flying start. In the former action a bent arm is powerfully snapped straight; in the latter, it remains bent and therefore lacks that essential extra snap.

There are three main overhead strokes: the defensive clears and the attacking drop-shots and smashes. Even though the clear is generally defensive, we will tackle it first because it is in some ways the simplest of the three – and we want early success. All strokes consist of three main phases:

1 Preparation As in all activities sound preparation is all important. In it are included *movement* to the shuttle and the *backswing* which leaves the striker actually ready to hit the shuttle.

2 Execution This is the vital make or break part of the stroke. It consists of the *forward swing* and the actual *impact* with the shuttle.

3 Completion If not as exciting as 'execution', just as important. The *follow through* launches the shuttle under control and on-target. The *recovery* sends you quickly on your way to the next stroke . . .

Defensive clear Now to turn these general terms into specific actions. First, however, understand the purpose of the clear. It is a shot hit high and deep to the back line of your opponent's court. High, partly in order to avoid early interception and probably anni-hilation, and partly to give you time to recover safely back to your base; deep, to the base-line itself to blunt the effectiveness of your opponent's returns. It is a get-you-out-of-difficulties, a good-enough-to-be-getting-on-with shot.

And it depends on *length* – a word to be borne in mind at all times. A shuttle, unlike a tennis ball, decelerates very fast. So a shuttle struck from the very back of the court will, when you receive it, be travelling shorter or more slowly than one struck from 0.6m (2ft) further forward. It will be more easily returnable.

So to the actual playing of a clear. You are, as we have already seen, mid-court in a position of readiness. As soon as you spot the flight of the shuttle to the back of your court you must obviously dance back two or three paces to position yourself sideways on so that if you allowed the shuttle to drop it would fall on your back foot. At the same time raise your racket directly upwards and drop it down over your right shoulder to scratch your back when the shuttle is just reaching its highest point. To do this your elbow is bent and your wrist cocked back.

So you are now sideways, with your weight on the back foot and your knees slightly bent. As the shuttle starts to drop throw the racket upwards with the heel of the hand leading. At the same time spiral your body upwards to put your full weight into the shot. Some 0.5m (18in) before impact uncock the wrist strongly but not fully, still hitting upwards. Make impact with a straight arm just to the right and above your head. The racket-head is still angled upwards at 45° to obtain height with maximum length.

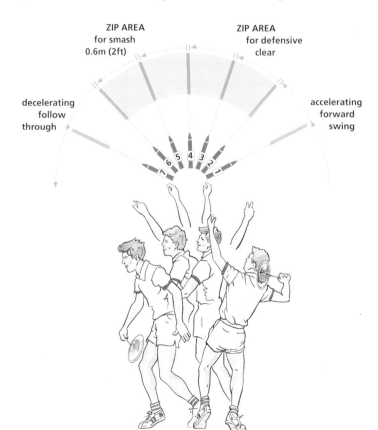

Points of impact and the 'zip area'

Now sweep the racket down to about waist height but keeping it on line to give the shuttle a last 'push' to its destined target area. Even as the racket is thus sweeping down, you, well-balanced, are heading back to base, hopefully to arrive there before your opponent can actually hit your return. A well-played shot – and you are ready to play another equally good one.

Enough 'do's' to last you some time. Concentrate on these and you won't need the following 'Don'ts'. However I include them to help you realize where, on occasions, you've gone wrong.

Don't fail to get behind the shuttle or your clear will be all height and no length. *Don't* delay your backswing until the shuttle has actually begun to fall. That way your shot will be hurried and lacking in power. *Don't*, above all other errors, push the racket forward instead of throwing it upwards. Lack of height and power will be the result. *Don't* fail to put your body into the shot as well as arm and wrist. *Don't* uncock your wrist too early or too late. *Don't* let your racket-head waver or your shot won't be on target. And *don't* stand there admiring your shot or you'll be in a whole heap of trouble with your next one.

Attacking clear There are circumstances and techniques when the defensive clear can be changed into an attacking clear. It is a slightly advanced stroke – not difficult in technique, but too rarely used at club level through lack of tactical forethought.

The circumstances for its use are when you are well-placed and on balance at the back of the court while your opponent, lured into the net by drop-shots, is still reeling back off-balance and there is an inviting gap behind him. Or, when your smash has proved unavailing and a well-dug-in defender is clearly expecting yet another smash. Or even when defensive clears of impeccable length have forced your opponent into a belated and apparently irreversible race to recover to his central base.

For deception and ease of technique play it exactly like your defensive clear. Except that . . . your point of impact is now more in front of your head and at impact your racket is angled upwards only very slightly. Your resultant punched shot therefore flies fast and almost flat to the unguarded space at the back of the court. You are well placed and in no need of time to recover so it is your turn to make your opponent hurry and force a weak return.

The drop-shot (slow) In contrast, the delicate and attacking drop-shot gives a big return for a small expenditure of energy. It is a shot played, like the defensive clear, from between the two back lines. Although it is hit gently it is an attacking shot because it is hit *down*, not up. Its aim, the converse of the clear's, is to draw your opponent as far forward in court towards the net as possible to create an opening behind him, or to attack him as he hurriedly retreats, off-balance. The nearer the shuttle can be dropped to the net, the further your opponent has to advance – and retreat.

Play it therefore exactly as you do a clear and so take your opponent by surprise. The only differences are that your point of impact is now just in front of your head, you arm speed is dramatically reduced in its last 0.5m (18in) before impact, and the shuttle is gently but firmly hit down to fall no further back in your opponent's court than his front service line. Anything deeper than that will present him with no difficulties in returning it or recovering to base. Gradually, learn to drop it shorter . . . and shorter.

Caution! The drop-shot at its best is a delicate and beautiful shot. As such it must be safeguarded by deception, for if it is spotted early for what it is, it has no defences. You must therefore make a *full* backswing and a forceful stroke to within 0.5m (18in) of impact. Above all you must hit *down*, and don't overuse the shot.

The drop-shot (fast) This is played exactly like the slow drop-shot except that it is hit a little harder to drop about 1.2–1.5m (4–5ft) behind the front service line. It is much used in mixed doubles when there is a lady ready waiting at the net for a slow drop.

The smash The most important and satisfying of the three overhead shots. It is the power shot, that scorches through your opponent's defence. It is the clincher of rallies, the winner of points, the climax of a dozen previous shots.

It is played with much the same action, the throwing action, which you have already mastered in the clears and the drop-shot. All three must be played similarly up to the last fraction of a second so that each is invested with deception.

It differs from the clear only in these respects. You must position yourself *further behind* the shuttle since you are going to take it earlier and some 0.5m (18in) in front of your face. At impact

THE ACTION FOR THE SMASH

the wrist fully – and powerfully – uncocks so that the racket face is directed downwards. And because of this downward sweep the follow through is longer, down past the legs. But not so long that the racket cannot be quickly brought into action again to kill off the weak reply elicited. On occasions your smash is only the first of a barrage, each eliciting a slightly shorter and shorter reply until after perhaps three or four you administer the *coup de grâce*.

'Don'ts' are mercifully few – but only because they have already been largely dealt with under 'the clear'. *Don't* be sluggish in your footwork. *Don't* attempt to gain power by brute strength alone; remember that it is best achieved by the perfect synchronization of each phase of the shot in a steadily rising crescendo of speed – by timing. And *don't* let the shuttle drop in the vain hope that you can hit it harder at head-level than at full-arm stretch.

Remember, too, that in these days of light racket manoeuvrability and fast reactions, speed alone will not always gain the day. To be fully effective it needs three allies. The first is *steepness*. The hardest smash hit flat but not downwards can be attacked, driven downwards. If it is hit steeply, by means of straight arm and crisply uncocked wrist, the return must be lifted. The second is *placement*.

The smash should never be a wildly swung blow: it should be directed to the inner hip, to elicit a cramped reply; or to a gap from which the shuttle will not be returned. And the third is *consistency*. It gains you nothing to achieve one rabble-rousing outright winner if the next two tear holes in the bottom of the net or spread alarm amongst side-line spectators.

Backhand strokes

We all have our weaknesses, and in badminton it is generally in playing backhand shots, i.e. those where the shuttle is struck on the left-hand side of the right-hander's body – with the back of the hand to the net. This is not as natural an action as that used on the forehand, and consequently is weaker and more subject to error.

The backhand therefore is a two-faced coin. Knowing it is likely to be a weakness, opponents will make a ploy of hitting the shuttle to your left. You must therefore regularly practise backhand strokes to eliminate such a weakness. Conversely, of course, you must hit to your opponent's left-hand side, especially in the rear court, rather than to his forehand side.

As a backhand stroke even when frequently practised is often still weaker than a forehand one, it is better to avoid playing such a shot at all when the shuttle is hit high and deep. This can be done in two ways: (1) by running round the shot and, (2) by playing round-the-head strokes.

Round-the-head strokes Too often a shot even a foot or so to a player's left seems to mesmerize him either into inaction or to a timid attempt at a weak backhand stroke. If you are in an alert position of readiness it is easy enough to skip or chassé a couple of paces to the left so that the shuttle is now just to your right and can be played forehanded and more powerfully. Quite simple, isn't it?

Even if the shuttle is 0.9–1.2m (3–4ft) to your left there is still opportunity to avoid using a backhand stroke. It is too far away for you to play it forehanded as just described. Instead you will play a round-the-head stroke in the following way.

Chassé, or turn and run, across court to as near its line of flight as possible. At the same time prepare your

THE ROUND-THE-HEAD SMASH

stroke normally by dropping the racket-head over your shoulder to the 'scratch' position. Now you are only one or two feet to the right of the shuttle and square to it. Make a final long sideways stride by placing your left foot well out to the left. Don't throw the racket normally (i.e. straight forward to the right of the head), because the shuttle isn't there. Instead, as you lean well out to the left, bring it across your head to hit the shuttle, still with the forehand face of your racket, 30–60cm (12–24in) to the left of your shoulder. Your forearm actually brushes the top of your head.

By placing the left foot well out to the left, try to maintain balance or you will be dangerously out of position. By thrusting off hard with it, make a quick recovery to centre court.

With this ploy you can play forehanded clears, drop-shots, or smashes, as previously described. However, you can dodge back-hand strokes only to a point; you can't eliminate them.

Backhand strokes in general First a few rough rules of thumb for all such strokes, before we consider them individually:

1 The basic grip may be used, but a specialized grip will probably give you added power and control. To achieve this hold the racket in the basic forehand grip. Relax that grip and with your fingers turn the racket some 30° to the right. You can now place your thumb flat along what is going to be the back bevel of the handle. This will give you extra leverage and control. Practise this change from forehand to backhand and back again off-court until it is automatic. In play, it should require no conscious thought.
2 The right foot is always placed towards the shuttle's line of flight.
3 A the same time bring the right hand near the left shoulder (arm bent; wrist cocked back) so that the racket may be thrown flat, down or up at the shuttle.
4 Begin the forward swing by thrusting the right elbow 'into' the shuttle, then wrist, and racket.

Let's start with the simple lob and work our way up to the crowning glories of the overhead strokes.

Backhand lob The lob is an underhand stroke used to return a shuttle which is well below tape-level, in the forecourt. Its aim is to hit the shuttle high and deep to the back of the court to give you time to regain your base against your opponent's attack.

Move to the shuttle taking a final long lunge so that you are not cramped and keep your back foot near base. Point the right foot at the drop of the shuttle. Bring the racket to the left side of the body with right hand by left shoulder, and racket, by means of bent arm and bent wrist, held vertically at shoulder level. Sweep the racket-head down with the elbow leading, the arm straightening and, in the 'zip' area, wrist uncocking to make impact just to the left of the leading foot. Let the racket flow with straight arm above head level on line with the target area. Recover quickly to your position by thrusting off strongly with the bent right leg.

Remember you are hitting the shuttle only just half the length of the court so 'lean on it', stroke it, rather than hit it. If the shuttle is dropping very near the net you will have to angle your racket face to give the shuttle the necessary lift to clear the net.

Backhand drive The drive is a splendid attacking shot, hit fast and flat generally down the side-lines. It is used mainly in mixed doubles by the male player.

THE BACKHAND LOB

THE BACKHAND DRIVE

All the principles previously mentioned apply again. This time however instead of diagonally facing the net you are head on to it. The right foot points directly at the side-line, slightly distanced from it so that the shuttle can be struck at full arm's-length. Right hand is again by left shoulder, but the racket shaft is horizontal to the ground and virtually across the shoulder.

Fling the racket-head at the shuttle, arm straightening, body turning, wrist uncocking, to make impact just in front of the body. If the shuttle is at tape-level the racket-head will be absolutely vertical to produce a flat, net-skimming shot. (If the shuttle is slightly below, the racket-head is very slightly angled up; if above, down.) Lean into the shot so that you can keep the racket-head square to the shuttle and flat as long as possible to drive it down the side-line. (To play a cross-court shot meet the shuttle 0.5m (18in) *in front of* the body and hit across court.) Follow through to above the right shoulder and, pushing on the right foot, recover quickly. Remember, do get that right foot across.

Danish wipe or Swedish swish These are a cross between drive and lob. Played from the back of the court, the shuttle is allowed to drop to waist height. Drive action is used but instead of a flat swing the racket is swept down then up under the shuttle to loft it right to the base-line. Use plenty of 'wipe', body action, and 'swish', wrist action. Its disadvantages compared with the overhead clear are that by letting the shuttle drop, downward angle and variety of shot are sacrificed. Worse still your opponent is given time!

Overhead backhand strokes
The most elegant and apparently effortless of strokes as they rely largely on use of the wrist and timing. But they need a

commensurate amount of practice. Clear, drop-shot and smash can all be played as with the forehand.

So, pivoting on your left foot, almost turn your back on the net (though still watching the shuttle carefully over your shoulder) and point your right foot to the left-hand, back corner 'box'. At the same time, right hand yet again to the left shoulder, arm bent, elbow up, wrist cocked so that the racket-head is roughly on a level with the small of your back. Bend the knees slightly, spiral the body upwards, snap the arm straight, uncock the wrist and make upward impact just in front of the head. There is very little follow through, the racket-head actually rebounding slightly. Since so much of the stroke's power is in the wrist snap, this must be very exactly timed – within the 'zip' area 0.5m (18in) each side of the impact point.

For the smash, impact is some 0.5m (18in) in front of the head. And as the backhand smash is very much less powerful than the forehand you should not attempt it from further back than mid-court, from where it can be an efficient snap-shot. As an alternative from deeper in court there is still the drop-shot, in which the wrist is gently rolled over to make impact in front of the head.

HOW TO PLAY THE 'DANISH WIPE'

PLAYING A BACKHAND CLEAR

THE BACKHAND SMASH

Side arm strokes (forehand)

The drive This is a side arm stroke played flat and fast down the side-lines. Its aim is to gain a weak return or a winner by driving the shuttle fast into a player's body or into a fleeting gap. It is used mainly by the male, from mid-court, in mixed doubles.

It is played with somewhat the same action as that used by a person skimming stones across water. To this end, chassé to your right then take a further long step across so that you are sideways on with your feet in line pointing at right angles to the side-line. At the same time prepare your stroke by drawing the racket back at shoulder height so that by bending your arm and cocking the wrist the racket-head is brought back almost between your shoulder-blades. Your body weight is still mainly on the back foot.

Fling the racket-head out towards the shuttle by snapping the arm straight and uncocking the wrist in the 'zip' area. But at the same time return your body square to the net and let your weight

flow into the shot and on to the front foot. With racket-head
angled slightly down if the shuttle is above the tape, and at right-
angles to the floor if it is level with it, make impact at full arm
stretch just in front of the body. This maximizes power and
minimizes the distance you have to recover to get back to base.

The push This stroke is played with exactly the same action as the
drive – for deception. But the shuttle is struck with only half the
force to drop between net-player and back-player. The 'power'
action hopefully deters the former from attempting to intercept.

The drop-shot This stroke is played threateningly like the drive
until just before impact when arm and wrist speed are both consid-
erably slowed down to hit the shuttle only just over the net.
Because the shuttle is travelling so slowly it may be necessary to
angle the racket-head slightly up to overcome the pull of gravity
tending to drag it down into the net. And again because of its vulnerable slowness of flight it should be played only when both
opponents are mid-court or the net-player is slow, off-balance or
positioned too far behind the front service line.

THE FOREHAND DRIVE

Net-shots

Net-shots are played *from* near the net, and often, very near *to* the net. They can be hit down or up. The latter, requiring a featherlight touch, may travel no more than an inch upwards and forwards and yet win a point outright as surely as a heavyweight smash.

Upward net-shots These shots are played as returns of drop-shots or of your opponent's net-shots. Your aim is twofold: to return them so close to the tape that your opponent cannot hit them down; and so tight to the net that your opponent will find it difficult to play the shuttle without hitting the net and, even if he does so, to get sufficient angle to hit it to a good length. A net-shot, therefore, ideally grazes the tape and topples immediately down touching the net as it falls.

To play these stand at about an angle of 45° to the net with the right foot forward. With racket arm extended and almost straight try and make impact as early and high as possible. Take the shuttle at tape-height if you can and it will almost bounce off your racket without any action by you. Take it a foot lower and it will need only minimal action, a delicate upward caress, not a blow.

The backhand net-shot: watching the shuttle intently on to the very strings

For all the delicacy, it is a perfect stroke in miniature, one played with back- and forward-swing and follow through all within a compass of a mere 23cm (9in).

If you are late in intercepting the shuttle, you will obviously take it well below tape-level. And if it is so tight to the net that you cannot play it without hitting the net as well, you will have to let it fall below the level of the bottom of the net. In these cases you will have to sweep it more strongly upwards.

Downwards net-shots Obviously it is far better to hit down for a fairly certain winner than hit up for a more problematical one. To be able to hit down you must take the shuttle earlier still. And to do that you must be on your toes, quick to spot a weak shot to the net, and bubbling with aggression.

To that end therefore stand, better still bounce a little, square to the net, with your racket upraised at tape-height in front of your right shoulder, in a 'frying-pan grip' or the basic grip.

The frying-pan grip almost speaks for itself! In it the racket is held square on, not sideways, to the net, with the palm directly behind the handle. It is good grip for dabbing down as it enables the net-player to play shuttles on either side, backhand or forehand, without changing grips. It does however necessitate a quick change of grip if an upward shot has to be played. It should never be used at the rear court as it inhibits use of the wrist.

With the grip decided on, all that is needed at the net is a dabbing action. You have no time – and no need of a full 'scratch' backswing, so do not bring the racket back further than your ears. Impact is a little in front of the body just above tape-height, when the bent forearm has been extended a little and the wrist has been uncocked. The latter action is essential if the shuttle is to be hit steeply down. Failure to use the wrist leads only to a flat and easily returnable push. Or, if struck with real venom, to the shuttle still gathering speed as it flies out over the base-line. Over-ambitious use can drag the shuttle down into the net. So aim for a happy medium that places it on the floor about mid-court.

Recovery of the racket-head is very important. You are hitting the shuttle crisply to a near target. If it is returned, it will fly back equally fast. So immediately the short follow through is ended, for fear of hitting the net, have the racket upraised again.

Return of serve

Just as important as the serve itself! If you serve well, particularly if you get the lift, you could well win most of the following rallies. If you return well, you make it very difficult for your opponents to score points. A very pleasing combination.

Position in court Your aim is to meet every serve, low or high, while it is above the tape. You must therefore so position yourself that you can reach both in time to attack them. A top-class player, very fit and agile, can stand right up to the front service line knowing that he can spring backwards and kill high or flick serves. This is your ideal too – but not yet. Remember that once you have developed a reasonably strong smash, serves to you will generally be low. So make certain you can meet those before they drop below tape-level. Stand, or rather crouch, 0.9m (3ft) behind the front service line. And, in the right court, within 0.3 or 0.4m (1–1½ft) of the centre-line to cover your backhand. In the left-hand court you will still be 0.9m (3ft) back but you will have moved your position some 0.9m (3ft) more away from the centre-line. Your aim here is to cover your weaker backhand to some extent but to be quite sure you can still attack anything down the centre-line.

In the final analysis only you, knowing your own speed, greyhound-quick or cab-horse slow, can decide exactly where you stand. Err on the side of optimism because you must be able to attack low serves. If you're caught by more than one or two flick serves you'll have to drop back – and hate it.

Stance It is important to position yourself exactly to be able to attack both low and high serves. it is equally important how you stand. You must be quick off the mark!

To that end take up a sprinter's starting position. Left foot forward, right foot stretched out behind in a long crouch. You are on the balls of both feet. That way you can push off quickly forwards from the back foot. Your left knee is well bent, your right rather less so. Your weight is on the left foot so that you are leaning slightly forwards, for that is the direction in which you will travel the majority of times. Your racket-head is held at head-level, slightly forward of the body, ready for instant action. Your left hand is at the same level, still further forwards. Look threatening!

THE RETURN OF SERVE STANCE

Return of the smash

We have seen that the smash is the most powerful shot in your armoury. And doubtless too in that of your opponent. So, how to counter it? Returning a shuttle hit hard and travelling fast demands several qualities – coolness, concentration, observation, fast reflexes and racket manoeuvrability. Sounds a tall order, but if you take one thing at a time it's not as difficult as it sounds. And there is great satisfaction to be obtained from nonchalantly returning your opponent's best thunderbolts.

Whenever you lift a shuttle to the back of the court (but do it as rarely as possible) immediately prepare for trouble. Too many players lack urgency – not panic, but urgency. And yet the shuttle will be whistling back at them in a split second.

Position and stance Coolly drop back to mid-court to take some of the speed off the shuttle and make your task a little simpler. Generally position yourself nearly square to the net but with the right foot slightly forward. Your racket, in a backhand grip, should be angled so that the head is up in front of your stomach – a likely target. In such a position you are immediately ready to counter shots straight into the body. And your racket-head is equidistant from shots either side, so leaving no glaring gap. Don't dig in to resist the 'shock', but rather be on your toes because your tricky opponent may not smash at all – but rather see if you are alert with a well-disguised attacking clear or drop-shot.

Watch that action Well positioned and armoured, you now concentrate solely on your opponent's action to try and spot early whether it's his action for smash – or drop.

    If it is the former, now observe his racket-head closely to see whether, at impact, it is aimed at your body, to the left or to the right. Then from his racket-head pick up the line of flight of the actual shuttle. And follow it on to your very strings.

The push or block If the shuttle is hit to one side of your body you have little time for any real backswing. Nor do you need it. For you merely place the racket to the side under pressure, just behind the body. Then, with wrist slightly forward 'block' the shuttle back, angled and fast enough to avoid net interception. The same applies to a shot aimed at your body which should be played backhanded. But the backswing will be limited – by your stomach.

The drive Playing just one type of return invites anticipation and interception, so learn other returns. This is virtually the same stroke as the push played with a little more backswing and therefore harder, which pre-supposes you are now spotting the shuttle earlier and so have time for that slightly longer backswing. It is hit fast either directly at the smasher before he has time to fully recover from his power-shot – or to the opposite side of the court.

Net-shot This is a third alternative. Played much as for the 'block' but the backswing is almost entirely eliminated. The shuttle bounces off the racket, held in a relaxed grip, to drop just over the net. Very useful against a player who stands back for the drive.

Crouch defence Contrastingly aggressive and only for those who like to take the fight to the enemy. All depends on your opponent's speed and steepness of smash – and your reflexes.

If his cross-court smash tends to be flat, move into the front service line, and crouch down diagonally opposite the smasher. You are now some 1.5–1.8m (5–6ft) further forward than the norm and the shuttle may well be travelling 32km/h (20mph) faster there than when further back even though it is on the longer cross-court line.

Make sure therefore that your racket is raised head-high even before your opponent strikes the shuttle. If you are frightened of being hit in the face, hold the racket in front of it, and look through the strings. At this close range you will have time only to 'dab' the shuttle down with a slight forward movement of the forearm and a slight uncocking of the wrist. It really is a 'kill or be killed' shot.

The lob A last resort. This is played like the lob already described though the long lunge is going to be unnecessary. Indeed it can best be likened to the high service. It demands quick reflexes and racket manoeuvrability because, from the basic defensive position of readiness, the racket must be swung back just behind the thigh. It is then swept down to meet the shuttle by the leading foot. Use of the wrist will help loft it to the back of the court – and with essential 'timing' minimize the amount of power needed.

But whichever technique is adopted nothing alters the fact that your opponents are still attacking. The status quo has not been altered. So, in defence your motto is 'Keep it flat! Regain the attack.' Don't base your defensive game on the lob – it's just too risky!

GAME TACTICS

Court courtesies

Badminton, like all other sports, has its code of good manners. In your early club days, members will ask you to play, not vice versa, or a Committee member, supervising a 'board system', will arrange your games for you. Later, when you make up your own games, don't ask the aces but rather players of roughly your own standard. When called, be ready and quick to go on court. But never walk across another court or even walk behind one when play is in progress.

Don't be afraid to tell your partner you are inexperienced. Without overdoing it, praise – 'Good shot' – or encourage your partner – 'Well tried'. And after a particularly poor shot of your own an occasional wry 'Sorry, partner!' doesn't come amiss. When you, or your partner, hits the shuttle into the net, accurately return it to the server. *Never* just scoop it back.

In matches it is customary to shake hands with your opponents at the end of a game but in club play 'Thank you, partner' suffices.

Badminton has always been a singularly sporting game. It certainly has no time for tantrums, excuses in defeat, recriminations as to the score, or disputed line calls. In regard to the latter remember you never query your opponents' line decisions on their side of the net. On your side, call quickly. If there is a slight doubt give it to your opponents; a reasonable doubt and ask if a let may be played. It is up to you to call your own slings or touches.

Even if you never become the club 'tiger', you can at least be a good sport, who never gives up and who is fun to play with.

General hints
(applying to doubles as well as singles)

1 By concentration and care avoid unforced errors.
2 If you are down in points, never be down in spirits.
3 Never show anger or despondency to your opponent; it's a boost to his morale, and it doesn't help yours!
4 Know the score after each rally.
5 Within the Laws and bounds of sportsmanship, slow the game down if you are losing, speed it up if you are winning.
6 Try to realize your errors of technique or tactics: and to spot and play on your opponent's.
7 If you creep up from 8-13 say, to 13-all, avoid the danger of unconsciously relaxing and finding yourself 0-3 down.
8 Similarly, at the beginning of the second game, decide on your tactics and then start away again at full pressure.
9 If you're winning easily, never ease up and let your opponent(s) have a few easy points. He (they) will play better and you will find it hard to get back into the saddle again.

Overleaf: In-depth play. Several matches in progress at once at the Yonex All-England Championships of 1993

10 Don't rage at net-cords against you or doubtful decisions by your opponents. You merely lose concentration and play badly.

11 In doubles, 'call' for your partner. If he is racing to play a shuttle he has little time to spare to see whether it is likely to be 'in' or 'out'. You have. So call 'Yes', if likely to be in; 'No', if going to be out; and 'Watch', if it's very close. Call early and sharply.

12 Take time at the end of the game, or even quickly between rallies, to point out an opponent's weakness you have spotted, or suggest an improvement in your own (or partner's) tactics.

13 Be scrupulously fair.

14 Fight to the last point whatever the score.

15 Win modestly, lose cheerfully.

16 In losing, learn. After every game, be a little badminton-wiser.

SINGLES

As a novice you will find singles an excellent form of practice. However, in a one-court club your opportunities to play singles will be few. Try very early – or last thing. Far better, if you can, to book a sports centre court for an hour's continuous practice.

In order to play such singles you must be more than averagely fit – though the very act of playing will increase stamina and fitness. And, hopefully, create a sound range of basic strokes. With only one player on each side, the tempo of the game is slower, more measured. You have more time to think your shots and the tactical plan is simpler in that you have only yourself to consider.

Preliminaries

These play their part. Warm up off-court before you start, as much to get the adrenaline flowing as to avoid pulled muscles.

If you have choice of ends, carefully note background for vision, floor for roughness or slipperiness, or possible 'drift' due to strong draughts or heating-fans in a big hall across, up or down a court. Some players like the best end first to gain the first game and win in two 'straight'. Others, perhaps more pessimistic, take the worst end first so that in the crucial third end-game they have the advantage of the best end to clinch the game.

In your knock-up, concentrate only on the singles strokes you are going to need. Conceal your weaknesses if you can. A quick show of force with withering smash or deceptive drop can be effective, but don't overdo it. Note your opponent's weaknesses and his strengths. Strive for concentration, length, consistency, and movement.

High serve

Remember that as you are playing within the bounds of a long, narrow court your aim is to run your opponent up and down it from corner to corner and to tire him and force weak returns.

To that end, the serve in singles is high and deep to the base-line which now, in singles, is also the back service line. From the right court aim a couple of feet to the left of the centre-line. This leaves a reasonable margin of error and cuts down your opponent's chance to cross-court disconcertingly. From the left court leave the same margin, or take the slight risk of a less likely cross-court shot by hitting to what you hope is a frail backhand.

Whichever target area you thoughtfully choose and observe, remember your *length* must be full – within a foot of the base-line. This should blunt your opponent's attack; his smash will lack penetration, his clears length, and his drop-shots, urgency. And you have also opened up the forecourt for attack.

Narrowing the angle If you do decide to serve out to either corner then instead of stepping straight back, step 0.3m–0.5m (12–18in) to one side of the centre-line; to the left if you have served to the forehand, to the right, if to the backhand. This is called 'narrowing the angle of return'. The theory is that the majority of returns will be straight. Therefore, if you have moved as I suggest, you will be nearer such a shot and therefore faster to its return. And, provided you have not moved too far, you will be able to move across quite easily to take a cross-court shot. This movement applies equally when you clear or lob.

Low serve

The one disadvantage of such a high serve is that you have generously broken a key badminton principle by lifting the shuttle, so giving your opponent the attack. Top players you will notice use this high serve much more sparingly because at their level their opponent can smash and clear effectively even from so deep in

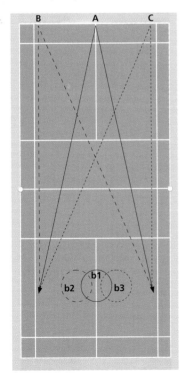

Narrowing the angle in singles: when the shuttle is hit to A, b1 is base; to B, b2 is base, to C, b3 is base

court. They therefore often employ a straightforward low serve to the T-junction. So, for variety, may you. But never give up a basic tactic too early or too often. An occasional change – and then a quick return to the high serve – can be unsettling.

If your high serve is having an off day in regard to length, a low serve is an essential variant. As your opponent has to stand further back to receive than he would in doubles he is unlikely to be able to rush it. He is therefore forced to lift, to give you the chance of attack either 'killing' his net-return or smashing his lob.

But there is another point to be noted. You are serving from a deeper base than in doubles so don't carelessly serve short. And remember that if you are weak backhanded a quick lob to that corner by your opponent can land you in deep trouble. So, in play, observe closely the results from low and high serves.

Flick and drive serves can be variants for the regular low serve. Your flick, remember, must fly some 1.2m (4ft) further, so try to keep it a deceptive flick, not an obvious hit. With a receiver standing further back a drive loses some of its surprise value. Use it therefore only on a weak backhand or into a generously large gap.

Return of serve

Return of serve is ever vitally important in that it sets the tempo of the coming rally. All that we have said previously as to position and stance applies, but to cope with a 0.75m (2ft 6in) deeper serve you will have to stand further back.

Of the low serve If it is high over the tape dab it down into a mid-court gap near the side-line. If it is tape-skimming, play a delicate net-shot to the corner of the net away from the server who dare not follow in as swiftly or far as he would in doubles with a partner behind him. If you are slow and your opponent follows in or has a weak backhand, then lift deceptively fast and just high enough to avoid interception to the back line – and look for a weak return.

Of the high serve If you have a strong clear, use it, to the backhand if your opponent is weak or sluggish and to the forehand if he covers his backhand side too much. By hitting to the forehand you open up the court, hoping to create a backhand gap that you can exploit next shot. If your opponent is strong from the forehand deep corner then obviously hit down, attack with a drop-shot to one of the front corners. In so doing you hopefully open up the back of the court for an attacking clear.

Of other serves Flicks should be smashed if of poor length, dropped if of good length, cleared high if you are off balance to give you time to recover. If your reactions are quick, a drive down your backhand can be lethally returned to body or gap with a round-the-head smash. If they are slow, a blocked, or dabbed drop-shot to the corner of the net is a safe reply.

War of attrition

Singles are not as forthrightly aggressive as doubles. In the latter with your partner covering the net you can afford to go all out for winners. In singles, on your own, you must be more circumspect for there is always a lot of court to be guarded. Singles, therefore, tend to be much more a war of attrition, of probing for an opening. So, although there is a No Man's Land when neither player is clearly on top, tactics are best divided under attack and defence.

Attack

Your main weapon is, of course, the smash. Use it sparingly for it is tiring, and should you not be on balance and in position, a quick return from your quick smash will leave you in desperate trouble.

Never, except as the rarest of surprise packets or if a gap is phenomenally large, smash from between the two back lines. It would be about as effective as hammering on a brick wall.

With the shuttle forced short by one of your previous succession of clears or drops, position and balance being good, go for a winner into a gap, though allow a margin of error for the down-the-side-line smash. A smash into your opponent's body, not comfortably either side on to his racket, will leave him cramped and force a weak mid-court shot you can finish off.

The slow drop-shot, for all its delicacy and lack of pace, is an attacking shot simply because, hit downwards, it forces a lift. It can be played from the base-line instead of an upwards clear. Played deceptively to the corners it can win a point outright, or, if it is tight enough, a lob short or into the net. Used in conjunction with the deep clear it can tiringly force your opponent in and out.

Overleaf: Rexy Mainaky and Ricky Subagdja of Indonesia, the men's doubles winners at the Yonex All-England Championships in 1996

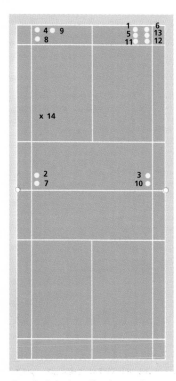

A typical singles rally. The numbers represent the sequence of strokes played

At this stage it is doubtful if your opponent will be quick or opportunist enough to risk an incursion into the net to kill it in mid-flight – always supposing you haven't generously signalled your intent by lack of backswing, grunt or grimace.

If you are off-balance, a high deep clear will at least maintain the stalemate status quo. If, on the other hand, it is your opponent who is off-balance after a lob or over-eager to get into the net then a flat, fast attacking clear over his head will send him reeling back too late or only able to make a very short clear.

What I have said of the forehand could apply to the backhand but, let's face it, your backhand may lack length, your smash, sting. If your overhead backhand isn't up to scratch don't disdain the lustier Danish wipe until it is. You must have length.

When your opponent plays a drop-shot, move in early to counter it with a tight net-shot – and another and another if need be. Don't be chicken by lifting to the back unless your opponent is too far committed to the net.

Games can be won in tight net play more often than on smashes. Such net-shots may force either a mis-hit into the net, or a return a foot above the tape that you can dab crisply down for a winner, or a half-court clear.

Be eager but not over-eager to score winners. Be prepared – and fit enough – to play long rallies until just the shot you need is played. Then go for the outright winner.

Do not play your shots to a pattern – for example, to each corner in turn, or more simply clear, drop, clear, drop, clear . . . play two, three, four successive clears then your drop – or vice versa. Even then you needn't alternate clears to each corner in turn. Keep your opponent guessing! It's both mentally and physically tiring.

Defence

Your range of strokes here is more limited, less clear-cut. The high clear and lob are never likely to gain you a winner but they will gain you time to get back to base, on balance, before your opponent can play his next stroke. Remember, height is a two-edged weapon: lots of it gives you time; the minimum of it, but enough to avoid interception, will hurry your opponent.

Length, too, is essential. Try and spare a glance at your opponent's feet. If his back foot is over the back line, the shuttle will fall just about on it. If it is only over the back doubles line, your lob or clear is short, and retribution will follow. Even if you cannot find time to notice this, do realize that if your opponent's smashes suddenly acquire the zing of a world-class player then that is due not to his sudden acquisition of genius but to your loss of length.

In returning any shot, but particularly in returning smash from rear court or dab from the net, 'be prepared'. Have your racket across body-target area, your feet moving in order to take avoiding action if there is time; and above all, your eyes watching opponent action and impact for early anticipation.

Your safest reply is a push drop-shot to the net. Alternatives? A wristy lob if the smasher is over optimistically following in, or a cross-court drive if he is off-balance.

MEN'S AND LADIES' DOUBLES

Ladies' doubles were once known as 'glassy eye', with male specta-tors making a quick dash for the bar. Rallies tended to be a series of interminable defensive clears with real action rare. Not so today. Anyone who has watched our ladies athletically battling it out will agree there's plenty of action from the likes of Alison Humby, Jo Muggeridge and Julie Bradbury.

Nevertheless, without chauvinism, it must be admitted that it is the even tougher men's double final that guarantees a full house and brings the crowd to its feet. See Gunawan leap a metre (3ft) off the ground, grunting ferociously each time as he hammers down thunderbolt smashes at imperturbable Jun Zhang who, with a flick of the wrist, whips them high back to an increasingly frustrated Gunawan. Then, with a grunt to outgrunt all grunts – a delicate drop-shot sends Zhenyu Min diving forward to retrieve it, somehow to inch it over the net where Mainaky prowls like a restless panther . . and 14,000 fanatical Indonesians chant 'Kill! Kill! Kill!'

One of the greatest moments in sport! Even at our more modest standard, level doubles is an exciting all-action game, and one in which you will always enjoy participating.

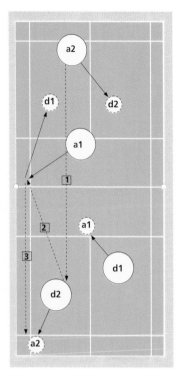

Changing position in men's and ladies' doubles. d1 and d2 move from defence to attack (a1 and a2) when a1 lobs d2's net-shot and d2 intercepts; a1 and a2 move from attack to defence (d1 and d2)

Court formations

Basically two are used: the partners switching from one to the other in the course of a rally.

In *defence*, where you lift to the rear court, you and your partner will each take up position near the centre of your service court in a 'side-by-side' formation. Rackets outstretched to the side cover the width of the court. Two long strides forwards or backwards enable you to return drops or attacking clears.

In *attack*, you will take up a 'back and front' formation. When, in their turn, your opponents lift to your rear court, the nearest player obviously moves back to strike the shuttle. Even as he dances back, his partner darts into the T-junction to fill a gaping void and to be poised there, ready, racket raised, before his partner even hits it. Thus, any weak return resulting from the 'back' player's smash can be attacked by the 'front' player before it drops below tape-height. This it would certainly have done had the smasher had to run in to retrieve it. The attack would have been lost.

Once the attack is gained this formation is maintained as long as either player is hitting down or playing so tight to the net that their opponents are forced to lift again and again . . . In this context even a delicate net-shot or a drop-shot that forces a lift is an attacking shot. The net-player must try to maintain the attack from the forecourt, his partner, from the rear court.

If either 'lifts' to the rear court with lob or clear, they have lost the attack, and are on the defensive. And they must consequently revert to 'sides'. But which side? If the net-player lobs, he is presumably under pressure, so he drops quickly back to the *nearest* service court. His partner can see this and equally quickly completes the defensive wall by moving into the other service court.

If it is the rear court player who clears, the alert net-player knows from his opponents' last shot – and the sound of his partner's feet – where the latter is. He darts into the other service court.

In theory it sounds simple enough. In early practice, when smashes are not hit down, clears are short, and net-shots high, the net-player has little time to think positionally. Hopefully, a safety reflex will send him scuttling back when faced with the prospect of a shuttle in the face from the upraised racket of a mid-court 'smasher' or 'net-dabber'. But with experience, and more accurate shots, the changes become automatic.

General tactics

The technique and general tactical aim of each stroke has already been described. Now only a rather more specific description is needed. Men's and ladies' doubles are played with basically the same tactics. But on account of ladies' comparatively weaker smashing and slower movement there are slight differences of approach which are dealt with at the end of this section.

At the outset both pairs take up back and front positions, each optimistic that they will gain the attack. Note how important is the server's partner's role. Crouched astride the centre-line, he must be able to return 'rushes' into the body, spring forward to take half-court returns early; or backwards to intercept lobs. Almost as important is the receiver's partner, standing mid-court and to one side of the receiver. When the latter leaps forward to attack the serve, he must be ready to maintain that initiative at the back with smash, drop or shots to the net.

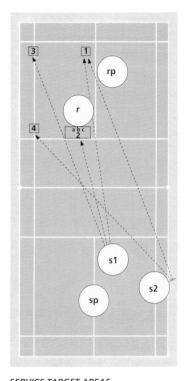

SERVICE TARGET AREAS
s1 = server's first option
s2 = server's second option
sp = server's partner
r = receiver
rp = receiver's partner
1 = drive, flick or high
2(a,b,c) = low (forehand, body, backhand)
3 = flick or high
4 = low

Serving

If points are to be won this is vitally important. The low serve to the T-junction area narrows your opponent's angle of return and, theoretically, gives you and your partner a better chance to intercept his return. If the receiver is lethal head-on, move your base a little to one side, though appreciating you've left a larger gap for a net return. Or serve to the side-line – though now, from the right court, you've made your partner's backhand vulnerable to attack and generally opened the angles. Always follow in thoughtfully on your low serve, watching your opponent's racket keenly, and looking for a net cut-off.

A well-disguised flick may temper your opponent's aggression. A flick to the centre runs the risk of falling into the wrong court. One to the side-line opens the angles but it does also drive the receiver from the centre, gives him a rather more difficult shot to play, and, with its extra distance, gives you the opportunity to flick more crisply, and therefore surprisingly, without overshooting the back service line. The drive should at least be tried tentatively to test a suspect backhand.

If nothing else is effective, a very high serve – or three, no more – may work by forcing mis-hits from a joyous and over-confident receiver who forgets that in receiving such a serve timing

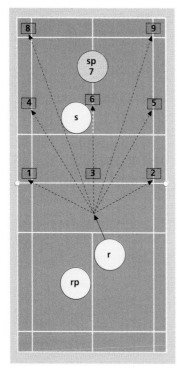

RETURN OF SERVICE TARGET AREAS
s = server
sp = server's partner
r = receiver
rp = receiver's partner
1,2,3 = target areas for net-shots
4,5,6 = target areas for half-court
    pushes
7 = target areas for fast rush to body
8,9 = target areas for fast rushes to
    back 'boxes'

is more difficult and the shuttle dropping vertically is harder to hit cleanly. Even try an angled flat drive following in for a weak return to the net. With all these variants, do be ready for a quick reply. Use both forehand and backhand serves.

Return of serve

You aim is to meet every low serve early – chest-high in front of the service line. So be fast and aggressive off a forward base. Don't, however, throw away a point by rushing into the net a shuttle that was above it when you moved but is below it when you hit it.

Dab low serves steeply down into knees or gap if you can. If not, use a tight net-shot to the corner most distant from the server. An admirable compromise for returning the shuttle tape-high or just below, is the deceptive half-court push. It must be fast enough to beat the incoming server yet drop short of the thrusting back player. Avoid the lob like the plague! If you must lift, then do it early, fast, deep and not too high – to the *backhand*.

In returning high or flick serves smash straight, unless you are definitely attacking the weaker player, and steeply, into an inviting gap, down the middle, or into the defender's inner side. Drops should be played to the middle, to cause doubt, or to the slower or less consistent player. Clears off a flick should be high to give you time to recover, and straight if you feel better equipped than your partner to deal with the return. In this server-receiver battle the odds are stacked in your favour. Gain the attack . . . and keep it.

Attack

Rear court This in mid-rally is the same as off a high serve. Anything short of the back service line should be smashed – and smashed again. Just occasionally, an attacking clear may catch out too firmly rooted defenders. From between the back tram-lines, play drops to force another lift, a shorter lift . . .

At the net If rear-court attack is to be effectively backed up you must have your racket up and be on the balls of your feet. Yes, literally, for you have only a split second to make you interception. Watch you opponent's action and racket-head at impact to get an 'early warning' start. Strokes played are much as in return of low serve: the dab and the upward net-shot. If the latter is returned with another net-shot, don't, in blind panic, lift. Keep it on the net – unless your opponent is altogether too good for you there.

Try not to be drawn right out to the side-line or you will be swiftly cross-courted. Reach for the line with foot and racket and you will still be placed to cut off a cross-court reply.

Defence

The best form of defence is attack. By anticipation and agility meet drop-shots early enough to turn them into lift-forcing net-shots, or even to hit them down for a winner. If lob you must, then fast, to a *length* and to the backhand. Be prepared for the occasional flat attacking clear – spring back and attack with smash or drop. Push back dabs from the net flat with quick reflexed arm action *away* from the menacing net-player.

The smash is the big gun you must spike. If it is sluggish and flat, move in and push, or drive flat and fast into the smasher's body or witheringly cross-court. Or move in further still, to dab in crouch defence. If it is powerful, drop back to draw its sting a little – but beware of drops to the now exposed forecourt. You will have to lob but at least swing your opponent from side to side – it's tiring and error provoking. Try and ensure length.

Ladies' doubles variations

Low serves will be returned tight to the net more often than rushed and fast lobs to the backhand may be played more effectively and safely. Since defence invariably over-rides attack, smashes should be steeper, more accurately placed and played from less far back. Flat clears, especially to a frail backhand, are useful alternatives. Drop-shots can be used with less fear of fast interception.

Net play becomes even more important. Tight net-shots may force the necessary short lift or be winners in their own right. As the back player's smash will not normally be strong enough to summarily end rallies, quicksilver foot work and fast reflexes are essential to administer the *coup de grâce*. Always keep alert!

MIXED DOUBLES

Mixed is a fascinating third game. With its accent on touch, deception, flatness of trajectory and new tactics, it is as different as chalk from cheese from the rougher, tougher hurly-burly of men's doubles. Let us, however, be under no illusions. Few ladies, if any, are as fast or powerful in rear court as a man. If they played there, the opposing man would run them ragged. So a system of court coverage counters this and capitalizes on the ladies' strengths of swift reflex, neat movement, quickness of eye and delicacy of touch. The lady plays, a little sheltered, 'at the net'; the man does the donkey-work 'at the back'.

The lady's role

Your male partner may well believe that he covers more than twice the court area than you do. But he forgets:

1 The lady at the net has half the time to see the shuttle that is travelling twice as fast!
2 She is cramped and is uncomfortably caught between an equally threatening female only a couple of yards away on the other side of a net she mustn't touch, and her male partner just behind her.
3 And, unlike the second male in men's doubles, there is no retreat from the net for her when a smash is threatened.
4 Moreover, she cannot see, only guess, what her partner is doing.

So, gentlemen, when your lady does make a mistake, do not, roll your eyes or sigh a sigh that can be heard a mile away.

Let's deal with her first – although always remember-ing that for all the clear-cut guide-lines of court coverage mixed is a partnership. Each player seeks to make an opening for the other; each tries to avoid putting the other 'on the spot'.

Position The lady covers across the court from side-line to side-line, and from net to front service line. Until she can smash and defend like a man she will be 'on base' in this area throughout the game – except when driven back with a flick or high serve.

This is a horrendous thought when you first play there with shuttles buzzing past you like angry bees. A sheer delight when you have found your feet – and touch – and are making winners off the increasingly frustrated men's best shots.

Your general base is on the T-junction of centre-line and front service line. There you stand, no bounce, on the balls of your feet, watching intently and intelligently your opponents' action to gain an early inkling of the shuttle's flight.

Serving The ability to serve really low to the centre, to 'narrow the angle', is a tremendous asset. It forces a lift to you or your partner, and puts you odds-on favourite to win the rally. If you serve to the centre, the shuttle, in theory at least, will generally be returned within your or your partner's reach. If you serve to the side-line, away from a menacing male racket, you make life difficult by 'opening the angles', i.e. by giving your opponent a chance to hit straight – or, suddenly, cross-court. If you serve thus from the right court you give your opponent a clear invitation to attack your partner's perhaps frail backhand. From the left, it is less dangerous.

As long as you are 'getting the lift', serve low. Your partner can't ask for more. As very occasional variants, try a probing drive to the backhand or a flick to the slower moving lady. Do not serve these any more than absolutely necessary to the faster-reacting man. As your partner has the whole width of a deep court to cover, it is not a good way to gain his approval. If you adopt 'crouch defence' you'll find it best to serve 'flicks' to the outside corners. And whether it is drive or flick be prepared for a very smart reply. Serve from as near the front service line as possible so that you can take net returns early.

Returning serve If you can also return service well (i.e. downwards) you will never lack partners. You simply must be aggressive, able to accelerate away from your alert position of readiness so that you can attack a low serve and flick alike. Bad low serves should be dabbed down steeply at the floor or into your opponent's body. Beware above all things of (1) the flat dab and, (2) the rising push straight on to your opponent's racket.

If you are not quite quick enough to hit down, a deceptive half-court push between the opposing team to what is known as 'the divorce area', is invaluable. If you really must lift, then a tight upward net return away from the server, not cross-court straight on to the oncoming server's racket, is the answer. If you do lift the shuttlecock, try not to do so aimlessly to your male opponent to hammer through you – and the floor. A quick, flattish, deceptive lift to the backhand is permissible – on rare occasions.

When your partner receives, you will stand in front of him, just to left or right. Later, when you have developed a worthwhile smash, he will ask you to stand a little to one side and behind him to cover the back of the court, if he is stranded at the net or needs to stay there to finish off the rally. When your partner serves there is a change. You stay in the left-hand court whichever side he serves from. This makes a reply to your forehand more likely.

Returning the flick serve effectively is vastly more difficult. Having bounced back to hit it you then have in virtually the same action to power your way back to the net. The man must stay at the back but if it is a match he will help out, by taking returns to the most distant third of the net.

You simply must not show the white feather by clearing. If you do, you will be a sitting duck as you quickly meet the shuttle again. Show this is all you can do and the man will relentlessly serve deep and you will become a battered target.

If you are on balance and have an accurate fast smash go for a gap and try and force a return to your side of the court. If not, a steep fast drop-shot to half-court will cause dissension in your opponents, force a lift, and give you more time to recover.

Serve and return are 60 per cent of the lady's game. Think them out and practise them!

Attack This is very similar to returning serve. All depends on your positioning, speed of foot and eye, and therefore ability to meet the shuttle early. Move a little to the side your partner is attacking so that you can step in to a cramped return. If he is stranded at one side of the court, or has smashed too straight and flat down the line so giving your opponent his eagerly sought chance to attack, move a little the other way, cross-court. Quick thinking is needed.

Shots below the tape return with tight net-shots to the corners. Keep it here – show who's mistress. With your opponent lured off-balance or too near the post play a cross-court shot, flat, fast to the opposite side-line. Those taken fractionally above tape-level can be best dealt with by the invaluable half-court. It draws the man in and pushes the lady back, forces a lift . . .

Defence Your duties here will depend on your abilities – and con-sultation with your partner. If your defence is weak he will leave you to crouch at the net while he shoulders the entire burden. If your eye is good he will ask you to drop back behind the front service line to return a cross-court smash with the crouch defence shot (This leaves your opposite front corner vulnerable, so decide with your partner who takes the drop there). With minimal backswing try and dab down into or away from the smasher. Only when you can cope with a man's smash will your partner ask you to drop back to 'sides' as in level doubles.

Combining Finally, remember you are a pair. Try to elicit lifted shots that his heaviest artillery can attack. Equally, avoid lifting and so leaving him desperately covering the whole court.

Have a clear understanding with your partner which shots you each take. If you can intercept half-court shots it will strengthen your partnership. But deciding what to take and what to leave can be as difficult as playing a shot. Never drop back far behind the front service line – as it is irritating for the advancing man to have an easy winner taken off his racket in a face to face encounter with an off-balance partner mid-court. Also, try not to intercept – then stop and suddenly leave it all to him. Take only those shots that you can effectively control.

The man's role

You have of course not skipped 'The Lady's Role' but read it as slowly and thoughtfully as she did. She too will read this so that she knows what her male partner might be doing.

Position A position of readiness astride the centre-line, or, if your backhand is a touch frail, a little to that side. Very much on the balls of your feet for you have a large area to cover. Very much too, eye on the shuttle. Do not hug the back of the court or there will be a gap in front of you; equally don't crowd in on your partner, or there is an even nastier gap behind you. Let's settle for 'equidistant' – an excellent word to bear in mind in badminton positioning.

Serving As, unlike in men's, you have no partner behind you, you must serve from deeper in court, say 1.5–1.8m (5–6ft) behind the front service line. Have your partner always in front to your left and as near the centre-line as she can by leaning to the left to avoid

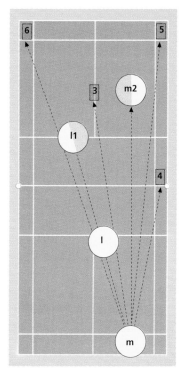

MIXED DOUBLES ATTACK AGAINST
CROUCH DEFENCE
l = lady
m = man
1 = smash at lady
2 = smash at man's right side
3 = smash between the two
4 = straight drop
5,6 = attacking clears

baulking your opponents. Yes, this certainly gives your opponents longer to see the shuttle but the opposing man is more chary of rushing in, with open court behind him.

'Low to the man', 'high to the lady' is no bad maxim at this stage – provided the lady does not pack a punch. If she does, it's low to both, to the centre, with a flick as an occasional mixer. A drive down the lady's backhand is a good idea – an angled drive still better provided you and partner know who takes the block to the net or the clear to the back. If played flat it can shake morale.

Returning serve Here the pattern is much the same as in men's – with two provisos. (1) Remember you have no one behind you so if a winner is not 'on', play a return, often half-court, that will give you time to regain base; (2) be less aggressive on the man's serve – and more aggressive on the lady's, where you can take a chance with your first return. If you can crunch it with a return straight at the face or the body you *may* well shake her morale.

Attack Understand first that neither you nor your opponents are going to lift unless forced to. Therefore much of the game is played flat, from mid-court, down the side-lines.

A fairly regular pattern emerges. A half-court return of serve to your forehand (or backhand). Take it high but probably below tape-level so your return is a deceptive half-court push. Your opponent, in the same boat, counters with the same move again.

This probing goes on until the opposing lady decides to chip in with a winner; or perhaps a half-hit return that you can hit cross-court to the far corner of the net – or at her. (Cast gentlemanliness aside and remember, if the opposing man is strong, play on what may be the much weaker lady. Have no qualms about it!)

If the lady does not intervene, you wait for a male push that is too high, too deep. Now you attack. Not with a smash, the shuttle is not high enough for that. But with a flat, fast drive down the side-line into the 'box', or across court, to the opposite tram-lines.

Beware of 'cross-courtitis'. It is infectious, exhilarating, but entirely predictable. If you play cross-court every time, as many club players do, your opponent knows what is coming. So use it sparingly only when (1) you can hit flat or down, and, (2) when your steady drip of straight, deceptive half-court pushes has brought both opponents to one side, and cleared the centre of the court.

On occasions the shuttle will be lifted. If the lift is short, smash – to the side-lines, or to the body to force a return to your eager partner. If the lady adopts crouch defence then smash steeply at her. Hit flat – and she may have it on the floor before you can blink. If it is deep, then a fast drop-shot (with a lady ready at the net, the slow drop is suicide). Again to the half-court No Man's Land. Another form of attack, if you think the opposing lady is slow, is to try and run her to and fro across-court with accurate flat net-shots.

Defence Here with two-thirds of the court to cover, you have problems – the reasons why neither man nor woman willingly lifts. Try and see the length of lob or clear – by looking at your opponent's feet. If it is really deep expect a fast drop – return it with push or net-shot. If it is short, cover the side to which the more likely straight smash will go. What now? If it's flat, push or drive it straight or cross-court according to your opponent's position.

Should it be the lady attacking you from the net with dabs to the body, be on your toes to side-step if you can. If not then it must be quick reflexed, straight-armed pushes through her, or at her, or net-shots to the corners.

Try always quickly to regain the attack with shrewd place-ments and a never-say-die determination. Remember how difficult is your partner's task. So play to set up winners for her; encourage and, if need be, console her and always consult her. A friendly post-mortem after a game will help both of you to know which of your shots helps your partner, and which puts her in deep trouble.

Useful
addresses

Badminton Association of England
National Badminton Centre
Bradwell Road
Loughton Lodge
Milton Keynes
MK8 9LA
Tel: 01908 268400

**The Badminton Umpires
Association of England**
c/o National Badminton Centre
Bradwell Road
Loughton Lodge
Milton Keynes
MK8 9LA
Tel: 01908 268400

**English Schools Badminton
Association**
National Badminton Centre
Bradwell Road
Loughton Lodge
Milton Keynes
MK8 9LA
Tel: 01908 268400

Scottish Badminton Union
Cockburn Centre
40 Bogmoor Place
Glasgow
Scotland
G51 4TQ
Tel: 0141 445 1218

The Badminton Union of Ireland
Baldoyle Badminton Centre
Baldoyle Industrial Estate
Grange Road
Baldoyle
Dublin 13
Republic of Ireland
Tel: 1 839 3028

Welsh Badminton Union
4th floor Plymouth Chambers
3 Westgate Street
Cardiff
Wales
CF1 1DD
Tel: 01222 222082

**Australian Badminton
Association**
P O Box 629
Kew 3101
Victoria
Australia
Tel: 3 9819 4300

**Canadian Badminton
Association**
1600 James Naismith Drive
Gloucester
Ontario
Canada K1B 5NL
Tel: 613 748 5605

**New Zealand Badminton
Federation**
PO Box 11-319
Wellington
New Zealand
Tel: 4 473 1062

Rules Clinic

index

Page numbers in *italics* refer to illustrations

index

Page numbers in *italics* refer to illustrations

A Ward Lock Book • Cassell • Wellington House •125 Strand • London WC2R 0BB

A Cassell Imprint • Copyright © Ward Lock 1998
All rights reserved. No part of this book may be reproduced or transmitted in any form or by any means,
electronic or mechanical, including photocopying, recording or any information storage and retrieval system,
without prior permission in writing from the publishers and copyright owner.

Distributed in the United States by • Sterling Publishing Co. Inc. • 387 Park Avenue South • New York NY 10016 • USA

British Library Cataloguing-in-Publication Data • A catalogue record for this book is available from the British Library

ISBN 0-7063-7688-9

Designed by Grahame Dudley Associates • Illustrations by Chris Rothero

Printed and bound in Spain by Graficromo S.A., Cordoba